CHURCHILL
HIS RADICAL DECADE

Malcolm Hill

OTHILA PRESS
1999

OTHILA PRESS LIMITED

58a Abingdon Road,
London W8

First published 1999

ISBN 1 901647 18 8

To those who aspire to a just democracy

Contents

Illustrations

Acknowledgements

My thanks are due to Catherine Feighan and Duncan MacAra for their editing to make the text readable and, I hope, enjoyable. I wish to thank Paul Turner and Sir Kenneth Jupp for their apt suggestions.

Quotations of Winston Churchill from *The World Crisis, Thought and Adventures, The People's Rights, The Second War, Great Contemporaries* and *Winston S.Churchill* by Randolph Churchill are reproduced with permission of Curtis Brown Ltd, London, on behalf of the Estate of Sir Winston Churchill. Copyright Winston Churchill.

Quotations from *Churchill As I Knew Him* by I. V. Bonham-Carter, published by Weidenfeld and Nicolson, are reproduced with the permission of The Orion Publishing Group.

The quotation from *Churchill – A Life* by Martin Gilbert, published by Heineman, is reproduced with the permission of the author.

Permission was sought in good time to reproduce quotations from the Chartwell Papers. However, none was granted nor refused.

The six photographs are reproduced courtesy of Hulton Getty and the two cartoons of Sir Francis Carruthers Gould are reproduced courtesy of the National Portrait Gallery.

Foreword

Any public figure is likely to be the object of a range of opinion stretching between something close to adoration, and something beyond abhorrence. 'To do justice to a great man', wrote Churchill, 'discriminating criticism is necessary. Gush, however is always insipid.'[1] But there is such a thing as general sensible opinion. Winston Churchill was no exception. During his long life he experienced a whole range of opinion concerning himself. But the judgement of the sensible is, and was, that he towered above the rest of his kind, an outstanding statesman and leader, 'a servant of Crown and Commonwealth'.

Not only in his native Britain, but in the 'free world' – meaning those countries where the degree of political, economic and personal freedom was sufficient to inspire them to resist aggression, and fight against the vicious barbarity and oppression of a nation who had submitted to a tyrant – Churchill's merit was eventually recognised. He was proclaimed as the man who converted a Britain, in which Oxford University, after heated and serious argument in the 'white feather debate', voted not to fight for King or Country, into a nation prepared to stand fast against the Nazis. After he became Prime Minister on 10 May 1940 the mood of the country underwent a sea-change. He offered only 'blood, tears and sweat', and the country was ready to accept him at his word. Within six weeks the evacuation of 225,000 British and 110,000 French troops from Dunkirk was accomplished. Anyone who was evacuated from Dunkirk will remember how even the Army's retreat was hailed as a kind of victory. The yachtsmen in their small ships became heroes; admiration for the Royal Navy and for the Royal Naval Voluntary Reserve with their motley collection of craft abounded; and the gallantry of the Royal Air Force had already been witnessed in Belgium. Indeed as Churchill wrote, 'There was a white glow, overpowering, sublime, which ran through our island from end to end.'[2] The nation was resolute to stand alone from June 1940 while Russia maintained its alliance with Hitler, and America stood aside. Without Churchill, Britain might well have capitulated to Hitler.

---

[1] *Winston Churchill Servant of Crown and Commonwealth* [in commemoration of his eightieth birthday]. p. 116
[2] P. Brendon, *Winston Churchill* p. 81.

But there was another side of Churchill which, eclipsed by the international acclaim he finally reaped in the Second World War, has now been forgotten. Malcolm Hill's book is timely. It deals with a period of Churchill's life in his first decade in Parliament when he was a doughty fighter for the poor and oppressed, a champion against monopoly, and against the privilege from taxation enjoyed by powerful interests. As a Cabinet minister in the later Edwardian period, he espoused measures for the relief of poverty: the eight hours Bill relating to work in the coal mines, a minimum wage, labour exchanges, unemployment insurance, old-age pensions, childrens' allowances against income tax, safety in mines, early closing and a half day off each week for shop assistants, books and entertainment for prisoners in gaols. Not only that, but he also devoted his boundless energy to a vigorous campaign for measures to eradicate these causes. His understanding of the causes of poverty, and of the means necessary to remove them, has never been approached by self-styled 'radical' politicians. One reform which he embraced was to enable society to recover the value which it had created.

The feeling for land as the basis of life, if it has been overlooked by most politicians, has not faded in popular estimation. It is based on biological and territorial imperatives. Men and women the world over are still prepared to die for their 'fatherland' or 'motherland', or just, as Hamlet said (IV. iv. 18 & 53), 'to gain a little patch of ground . . . even for an eggshell'. Walter Scott could say:

> Breathes there a man so dead
> Who never to himself hath said
> This is my own, my native land?

The astonishing thing is that this spirit should have survived in the landless, pressed men who fought at Trafalgar, and the common soldiers and sailors of the two World Wars, few of whom were in a position to echo Pope's praise of self-sufficiency:

> Happy the man whose wish and care
> A few paternal acres bound,
> Content to breathe his native air,
> In his own ground.

Churchill espoused the relief of poverty with as much enthusiasm as he upheld reform to eradicate poverty by removing the obstacles to people supporting themselves by their own efforts. His friend, Lord Birkenhead, gave an accurate insight into Churchill's character when he described him as 'a bewildering complex'. But Churchill was reflecting opinion in the country which was undecided whether to deal radically with causes, or whether merely to mitigate their effects. However, when at the fore-front of the campaign to introduce a just system of taxation Churchill was, however, surrounded by a Cabinet who had little understanding of how the taxation would have effected society. Though it was quite evident to a few ministers, including Grey and McKenna, who knew well how it would affect landowners., it became evident during the interminable debate on the Finance Bill that *parturiunt montes: nascator ridiculus mus* – the mountains in labour, produce only a ridiculous mouse. When enacted it became clear within a short time that it would have to be repealed, for it could not have achieved the objects which Churchill and others had intended. As reform was aborted, the mitigation of poverty became the only political alternative. That pattern was followed throughout the twentieth century, without thought of the cause of the poverty which obliged able-bodied individuals to pay Government in order to receive pensions; health, social security and the rest. These were very provisions which they could not afford during a life-time of work for themselves and their families. Churchill attempted to restore to the individual the ability to work towards prosperity.

The Western World to-day presents a picture of mass poverty and great individual wealth standing side by side with no understanding of each other. It is the picture Jesus of Nazareth painted of Dives, the rich man, clothed in purple and fine linen, faring sumptuously every day, and Lazarus, the beggar laid at his gate full of sores and desiring to be fed with the crumbs which fell from the rich man's table. It is the picture in the media of the wealth of America's three richest men equalling or exceeding the wealth of each of forty-eight poor nations: and of the wealth of the richest of the three equalling the wealth of 105 million other Americans.

Tremendous misplaced energy has gone into changing this situation by political action, which has failed miserably. Such thinking has produced only partial relief, euphemistically called 'welfare', financed from an unbearable burden of taxation which falls most heavily on the poor it is supposed to relieve. In fact, it degrades the poorest into a condition of dependency and despair in which they are not looking after themselves.

The choice between reform or mitigation is the theme of this book. It is a theme which should give us pause in our assessment of the politics of to-day: politics without gravitas, highlighted with fine words and slick slogans, but lacking sound reasoned argument for an effective remedy. Churchill would have destroyed all these in simple, forthright words appealing to the innate sense of justice possessed by everyone.

As things turned out Churchill had to devote himself to the defence of his country in the two World Wars. Peacetime concerns had to be set aside. In the coalition government which he headed in the Second World War he even allowed the Army Bureau of Current Affairs to promulgate a mild socialism. Many a junior officer detailed to instruct the troops in this propaganda must have been made aware of strong feelings in the ranks against the idea of high rise flats and state payment for all needs 'from the cradle to the grave', which was contained in the hand-outs. But it was all done to improve the morale of people who were to fight for a country which was owned not by them. It is a great irony that in laying the foundation of the welfare state, and in the propaganda by which he hoped to inspire the soldiers, sailors and airmen of the Second World War, Churchill sowed the seed for his ejection from office in the post-war election which brought a socialist government to power.

Sir Kenneth Jupp
Welwyn
October 1998

Introduction

In British history there have been few ministers who have spoken as directly to the people about the distribution of wealth and been so well understood by them as Winston Churchill. He had a gift of understanding their needs and expressing their aspirations.

Churchill proved himself a great statesman in peacetime. That fact has not been readily acknowledged. His first decade in Parliament, from 1901 to 1911 was arguably his finest in peacetime. It cannot be dismissed as his wild youth. For in that time he progressed from the back benches of the Conservative Party, crossed the floor of the House of Commons to the Liberal Party, was invited into government by Sir Henry Campbell-Bannerman and later ascended to the forefront of Asquith's cabinet and became Home Secretary.

The industrial revolution of the nineteenth century had been built on unsteady foundations. While it had produced great strides in technology and growth in population, it had been accompanied by widespread poverty. It was a splendid adventure for the successful entrepreneur, for the independent artisan, but for the mass it was toil and for them its most prized reward was survival only. Reform was desperately required.

Churchill entered public life at the beginning of an unusual decade. The passing of Queen Victoria in 1901 finally eclipsed the orthodoxy of mind that had prevailed throughout the previous century. As the nineteenth century drew to a close, the conviction which had sustained it was weakening.

Churchill played an influential role throughout the decade. He preferred political principles to party policies and embraced grand ideas with fearless and tireless enthusiasm. He abandoned the Tory Party, which he felt had become obsolete, in order to adopt the Liberal whip. Immediately he was accepted into the vanguard of Liberal thinking. After the landslide Liberal victory of 1906 he joined the government. Two years later he entered cabinet. Unfortunately, Campbell-Bannerman died after only two years in office and the complexion of Liberalism changed after his passing. Until his death in 1908, the new century seemed set on a path of reform of the unjust distribution of wealth. Yet by the close of that first decade a wholly different pattern of political action had been adopted. Reform of economic causes had been abandoned in favour of social mitigation of the effects of those causes. This marked a profound change of political attitude.

The new Liberal Prime Minister, Herbert Asquith, had no creative political imagination. He allowed Lloyd George, his Chancellor of the Exchequer, to formulate government policy. Lloyd George was a dazzling performer, but no political thinker. Unfortunately Churchill became his admiring lieutenant. Together they devised popular schemes for national insurance against unemployment and sickness, labour exchanges, schemes against 'sweated labour' and the like, without thought of the reason why the great majority of society found themselves in such a condition of poverty. Their policies became the foundations of the Welfare State.

After 1908 Churchill put himself in the hazardous position of advocating both the reform of the causes of poverty and at the same time leaving the causes alone and mitigating their effects. He was convinced of the need for reform by his political thinking, but his love of the limelight persuaded him to pursue popular measures of mitigation. He had shown from 1904 to 1908 a thorough grasp of the reforms, but as he came under the mesmerising influence of Lloyd George he forgot them.

The single measure which indicated most clearly both the strength and the weakness of Churchill's position was the budget of Lloyd George in 1909. The Budget pretended to effect reform in the distribution of wealth, but its architect failed to understand either the malady to be reformed or the nature of his own provisions. It was a poor Budget and it failed utterly to achieve its pretended goals. However, while it was passing interminably through the Commons, Churchill was making grand speeches about the justice of reforms, which were not contained in the Budget before parliament.

Retreat from this precarious position was necessary to maintain his political reputation. After 1911 Churchill dropped his zeal for reform of the distribution of wealth. He pressed instead popular ideas of mitigation. However, up to the end of his life, Churchill did not disown the ideas of his early Liberal speeches. Years later he once described to Lord Linlithgow the Liberalism of the early years of the century as 'vague and mild'. Most certainly, it was neither.

Indeed the climate of political thought had fallen victim to the First World War. It has failed to recover since. Sentimentality drives out justice and individuality becomes inconvenient, whereas they were once pillars of society In the war politicians became intoxicated with control of society and the liberty, which had arisen of itself in a more liberal climate of thought, disappeared during the build-up of the War.

Much can be learnt about economic liberty from Churchill in the decade up to 1911, such as the relationship between the individual and society, the distribution of wealth, the meaning and extent of private property, the principles of taxation, the degree of civil rights and the duties of government. It is necessary to discriminate between the statesman determined to reform the causes of poverty and the politician, who courted popularity by mitigating the effects of unrelieved causes. The purpose of discriminating between reform and mitigation is to learn about grand political ideas, which may yet inspire people to abolish the causes of general poverty in society. In the first decade of the twentieth century Churchill believed in fundamental economic ideas which operated as two blades to cut through problems due to economic injustice.

First, he proclaimed free trade as a perennial economic order. He saluted the example of Richard Cobden, the nineteenth-century pioneer of this order. Cobden warned frequently that tariffs were the breeding ground of bayonets. Free trade is of crucial importance today, as the world retreats behind protectionist ramparts which divide the globe into groups, such as the European Union. Such groups are built on molecules of regulation and bureaucracy.

The second problem which dominated Churchill's political thought was taxation. It was a key, he believed, which determined the distribution of wealth and should rest on justice and on a clear division between private and public property. The question of taxation depends upon a division between public and private property. This division lies deep, as it were, near the foundation of society; it is not concerned with the ceaseless and ever-changing traffic of its surface. Churchill was clear and emphatic on this division.

The exercise of political power without regard to justice is dangerous to liberty and, ultimately, to the institution of democracy itself. If a democracy is not prepared to look at poverty as a communal disease, then no democratic institution will be able to remedy it; democracy will not save a nation from the scourge of poverty.

Churchill was a political figure out of step with the traditional picture of Edwardian Britain. It is often portrayed as an interlude of elegant luxury at the centre of a large Empire. There was much evidence that the richer elements lived a champagne life with parties and countless diversions at tables or outdoors. The music of Sir Edward Elgar typified the decade. Some of it was used in imperial celebration but most of it was the music of a great composer who came to loathe being identified with imperial pomp.

Indeed, as a grandson son of a duke, Churchill might be supposed to have imbibed these pleasures. But his mother was an American and he held himself aloof from British life as experienced by his aristocratic contemporaries. For example, he held public schools and their ethics in a certain contempt.

He possessed a rare trait in politics; he could think for himself and he was fearless in expressing himself. Soon he connected with the real issue of the Edwardian decade. It concerned the evident injustices of Victorian society. He could see that the rich were few and the poor were many and that luxury represented the cream floating on the lifeless liquid which was the milk of the mass of society. In the previous century wealth was to be reaped by the entrepreneur but poverty was the recompense of the workers and consumers of their enterprise. The urbanisation of an increasingly greater part of the population throughout the Industrial Revolution had exposed the failure of the Poor Law, which had been the ineffective sticking plaster of society for three centuries. Churchill quickly gasped the cause of poverty.

That was a large step which few, very few, figures in politics have taken. It sounds simple to find out the cause of a problem. But the mere suggestion that poverty has a cause, that it is due to injustice and that it can be removed by parliament is too radical for a political party to advance seriously. They cannot afford to disturb vested interests. The individual member who can think and set party at nought is more important than an entire parliament of pedestrians. He may be able to do little but that has never been an excuse for a member of parliament not to think. That is the reason why, for example, a plumber can proceed to the cause and put right the fault at source. For in doing so he disturbs nothing apart from the fault. Political reality is more complicated.

Now it seems absurd that there was any resistance to the idea that the earth was round or revolved round the sun. Yet after at least seven centuries of uninterrupted continuance the cause of poverty remains a political taboo. Parliamentarians prefer to talk about anything but that. The radical is derided as a crank, indeed a dangerous one. The British people want, as Churchill remarked, 'business as usual'. They tolerate political intrigue, political boredom, political incompetence and they will allow the odd lie. But they do want not education in political thought, they do not want the full development of democracy and the one state they absolutely refuse to even consider is one of economic justice.

Unless the cowardice of the people to face realities like poverty is understood, it is impossible to appreciate the courage which Churchill showed at the outset of his political life and the rare achievement of his stand. It has not happened often that a minister of the crown has spoken with impassion and striking eloquence in parliament and in the country about a just distribution of wealth.

However, life is a complicated business. Unless there has been universal agreement about letters, dates, and arithmetic, life would be a matter of managing daily chaos. Because there is no aspiration in the British people or their parliament for economic justice there is political confusion of a kind that resembles a circus of lunacy. Churchill stood at first for the reform of an unjust distribution of wealth and against an unjust system of taxation. Taken together they constitute, arguably, the profoundest reform in Britain, apart from that which secured the freedom of speech. However, that grand endeavour led to results other than had been intended. The Edwardian decade was not just the passing of imperial pomp, by which it is often characterised, but it was also a critical period for the unfolding of the twentieth century in peacetime.

1

Parliamentary Debut
1901–3

Winston Churchill, while a child, met Sir William Harcourt, an aged Victorian statesman. At one point in their conversation young Winston asked, ' "What will happen then?" The old man replied, "My dear Winston, the experiences of a long life convince me that nothing ever happens." "Since that time it seems to me", wrote Churchill, "nothing has ever ceased happening." '[1]

On 14 February 1901 Winston Churchill entered Parliament as the Unionist, or Conservative Member for Oldham, after winning the seat in the General Election of 1900, the Khaki Election, by a majority of 222 votes. He joined the back benches of the Unionist Party, which had been in government since 1895 under the premiership of Lord Salisbury. Churchill had recently returned from South Africa. He was adopted for Oldham within five days of embarking at Southampton. The Boer war was still in progress there. He was twenty-six and already well-known outside Parliament for having escaped from the Boers in December 1899. At Westminster he was also known as the son of Randolph Churchill, who had briefly been Chancellor of the Exchequer in 1886. However, he resigned before presenting his first Budget.

In the weeks after his electoral victory, before taking his seat in the House, Churchill embarked on an exhausting lecture tour of England, America and Canada. He earned the sum of over £14,000, which was useful to a politician at a time when members of Parliament did not receive any salary.

While he was in Winnipeg he heard that Queen Victoria had died and been succeeded by her son Edward VII, aged sixty. Edward had been a playboy, with a passion for horses, yachts, parties and women. In 1870 he had been cited in a divorce case. Victoria considered him too frivolous and his critics considered him more plainly as 'fat and vulgar'. Winston wrote to his mother, 'I was curious to know about the King. Will it [his reign] entirely revolutionise his way of life? Will he sell his horses or scatter his Jews or will Reuben Sassoon be enshrined among the crown jewels and other regalia? Will he

---

[1] Winston Churchill [WSC], *World Crisis 1911–14* p. 26.

become desperately serious? Will the Kepel be appointed 1st Lady of the Bedchamber'.[1]

The King's style of dealing with matters was straight forward. He was more interested in people than in ideas. He tended to rely on the professional judgement of his ministers and was bored by detail. A courtier, Lord Esher, commented 'I do not believe that he ever has an original idea. Probably a man who spends his time talking between eight in the morning until past midnight has no time for thinking'.[2] Balfour, his minister until 1905, recorded later that the king 'never made an important suggestion of any sort on large questions of policy'.[3] He had tireless energy and settled his affairs before retiring at night.

Churchill recalled his introduction to the House of Commons:

> The whole meeting rose and shouted at my entry. With his great air [Balfour] presented me to the audience ... I was twenty six. Was it wonderful that I should have thought I had arrived? But luckily it is not so easy as all that: otherwise we would get to the end too quickly.[4]

Churchill soon established himself. No sooner had he arrived in Parliament than he resolved to make his maiden speech, which he described as 'the supreme ordeal' for the new Member. He contemplated it with 'awe as well as eagerness'.

> I need not recount the pains I had taken to prepare, nor the efforts I had made to hide the work of preparation. Within four days of his arrival in Parliament Churchill was waiting to catch the Speaker's eye. The war in South Africa was his strongest subject. He spoke after dinner from the seat above the gangway behind the Government front bench, from which his father had made his resignation speech. 'Mr Lloyd George spoke ...', Churchill recalled. 'He announced forthwith that he did not intend to move his amendment, but instead would speak on the main question ... I constructed sentence after sentence to hook on with his speech after he had sat down. Each of these couplings became in turn obsolete. A sense of alarm and even despair crept across me ... Then Mr [Thomas] Bowles [sitting next to him] whispered, "you might say instead of making his violent speech without moving his amendment, he had better have moved his moderate amendment without making his violent speech." Manna in the wilderness was not more welcome! It fell only just in time.[5]

With his opening remarks falling into place, his maiden speech was

[1] R. S. Churchill, *W. Churchill* vol 1 p. 543.
[2] G. Plumptre, *Edward VII* p. 149.
[3] M. Egremont, *The Life of A.J. Balfour* p. 148.
[4] WSC, *My Early Life*, Ch. 28.
[5] Ibid.

appropriately launched on 18 February 1901. He was able to develop his arguments. It was applauded as a triumph.

But one passage was considered a little risqué. 'If I were a Boer I hope I would be fighting in the field'. For though he had fought them and been imprisoned by them, he respected them as a noble enemy. Joe Chamberlain, a leading Tory, had whispered to his neighbour, George Wyndam, the former Irish Secretary, 'That is the best way to throw away seats!'[1]

He won warm applause, however, from the Liberal benches for his humanity towards the Boer farmers. He was generous to the spirit of enemies. He urged that military rule should be replaced as soon as possible by a civil administration.

He referred to the memory of his father, who had inspired him to enter the House. The filial devotion is the more touching when it is remembered that his father had treated him badly in childhood.

> I cannot sit down [he concluded his speech] without saying how very grateful I am for the kindness and patience with which the House has heard me, extended to me, I well know, not on my own account, but because of a certain splendid memory which many honourable members still preserve.

Churchill's own verdict on his performance was one of modest satisfaction. He had reached the other shore and had 'scrambled up the beach, breathless physically, dripping metaphorically but safe'.[2] Years later he remembered it as a 'terrible, thrilling yet delicious experience'.[3]

He received tributes in a speech next day from Sir Henry Campbell-Bannerman and Herbert Asquith, the Liberal leaders on the opposite side of the House. Asquith had revered Randolph Churchill and he was friendly to Winston from his entry into the House. His daughter Violet remembers her father's 'interest, verging almost on excitement, at Winston's arrival' He was their guest overnight when he visited Asquith's constituency to give a lecture on his experiences in South Africa in 1902. As Asquith once told his daughter, '[Winston] is an original and a most extraordinary phenomenon'.[4] He was introduced to Lloyd George, another Liberal minister and the meeting marked the beginning of their long 'association which persisted through many vicissitudes.'[5]

> At the very outset and in the first month of my Parliamentary life, I, who could hardly string ten words together spontaneously, managed to

---

[1] Ibid.
[2] V. Bonham Carter, *Churchill As I Knew Him* p. 85.
[3] R. S. Churchill, *Winston S. Churchill* vol i p. 12.
[4] Ibid 76.
[5] Ibid p. 240.

engineer and deliver at least three speeches which held the attention and obviously commanded the interest of a none to friendly an assembly. And not many people guessed how little spontaneity of conception, fullness of knowledge, or flow of language there was behind this fairly imposing façade. These methods are not to be recommended to those more brightly armed with natural gifts.[1]

Churchill's biography of his father, Lord Randolph, was published five years later. It was widely acclaimed and sold about 11,000 copies within three years. He received £8000 advance, which is a considerable figure in modern terms, when discounted by eight decades of ruinous profligacy in public finance and its consequent inflation. Violet Asquith once asked her father how Winston compared with his father, whom he had admired greatly. 'You can't compare them. Randolph was irresistible. He had incomparably more charm, more wit. 'But', he continued, 'Winston is by far the better fellow.'[2]

Speaking of the demise of individuality in society, Churchill wrote in the biography:

The late Lord Randolph was one of he last of the old school of politicians. His view was that gradually a man came to represent something in the Country, a certain share of public affection and confidence and could not surrender a part of his freedom of speech & action unless he exerted in return, as a Member of the government, a proportionate influence on public policy. This was why he refused for three weeks in 1885 to take office unless his conditions were met. That was why he resigned in 1886 on a matter of principle of economy – a very unpopular matter.[3]

Churchill showed his command of the written language in the biography:

Alike in the glare and clatter and in the silent diligence of a public department he found equal to all the tasks which are laid upon an English Minister. If he was thus armed and equipped at thirty-seven, what would he be at fifty? Who could have guessed that ruin, utter and irretrievable, was marching swiftly upon this triumphant figure; that the great party, which had followed his lead so blithely, would in a few months turn upon him in abiding displeasure; and that Parliament, which had assembled to find him so powerful, would watch him creep away.[4]

[1] WSC, *If I Lived My Life Again*, p. 5.
[2] V. Bonham Carter, *Winston Churchill As I Knew Him* p. 19.
[3] Chartwell Papers 9/13, 43.
[4] WSC, *Lord Randolph* [1907 edn] p. 569.

Randolph Churchill had threatened to resign over the level of military expense and Lord Salisbury, the Conservative Prime Minister, refused to be bluffed and in 1886 accepted his resignation. When asked if he would have him back, Lord Salisbury remarked 'When you have got rid of a boil on the neck, you don't want it back again.'[1] The threat had been written on royal letter-paper while Randolph had been staying at Windsor Castle. Queen Victoria thought it impudent that her paper should have used for political purposes. After he resigned, Randolph went into political decline and within a few years syphilis, then incurable, hastened his mental derangement and death at the age of forty-six in 1895.

Churchill had been treated badly as a child by his father. 'Few fathers', wrote Churchill's cousin, 'have done less for their sons. Few sons have done more for their fathers ... perhaps the greatest filial tribute in the English language.'[2] Although Randolph Churchill had been a poor father, he had set his son Winston a benchmark of political achievement. Shortly after his father's death in 1895 Winston had written: 'All my dreams of companionship, of entering Parliament at his side and in his support, were ended. There remained for me only to pursue his aims and vindicate his memory.'[3] As he entered Parliament in 1901 the memory of his father spurred Churchill on to ascend the political heights. It was like a standard raised before him. In his first two years in the House he was concerned with a variety of issues: mainly the war in South Africa and military matters.

In the 1902 session, alone among Tories, he opposed Brodrick's reforms of the Army. He described them as 'extravagant, unworkable '. In his speech Churchill 'had raised the tattered flag of economy and retrenchment' – borne briefly by his father. It was his first major speech in the Commons. First he attacked the expenditure on the Army.

[I]f this vast expenditure on the Army were going to make us absolutely secure ... I would not complain. But it will do no such thing. The Secretary of War knows ... that it will not make us secure, and that if we went to war with any great Power his three corps would scarcely serve as a vanguard. If we are hated, they will not make us loved. If we are in danger, they will not make us safe. They are enough to irritate; they are not enough to overawe. Yet, while they cannot make us invulnerable, they may make us venturesome.

Then he turned to the Navy. It was being substituted by the expense on the Army.

---

[1] A. G. Gardiner, *Prophets, Priests and Kings* p. 108–9.
[2] S Leslie, *End of a Chapter* p. 116.
[3] V Bonham Carter, *Winston Churchill As I Knew Him* p. 23.

This new distrust of the Navy, he continued, this kind of shrinking from our element, the blue water on which we have ruled so long, is the most painful symptom of military hydrophobia with which we afflicted. Without a supreme Navy, whatever military arrangements we may make, whether for foreign expeditions or home defence, must be utterly vain and futile. With such a Navy we may hold any antagonist at arm's length and feel ourselves in the meantime, until, if we find it necessary, we can turn every city in the country into an arsenal, and the whole male population into an army.

He concluded his speech with a rhetorical climax.

There is a higher reason still. There is a moral force which, as the human race advances, will more and more strengthen and protect those who enjoy it. And we shall make a fatal bargain if we allow the moral force which this country has so long exerted to become diminished, or perhaps even destroyed, for the sake of costly, trumpery, dangerous military playthings on which the Secretary of State for War has set his heart.[1]

So impressed was the journalist Henry Massingham that he wrote in *Pictures From Parliament* that, 'in its elevation of purpose, its broad conception of national policy, and in the noble and delicate movement of its closing sentences, I recall nothing like it since Gladstone died ... in years to come its author should be Prime Minister – I hope Liberal Prime Minister'[2]

Two years later Churchill was involved in a group called the 'Malcolmtents', young protesting member so named after Ian Malcolm, in a another attack on military expenditure and when Brodrick left the ministry shortly afterwards, the principles of his policy were reversed.

In the next parliamentary session Churchill attacked the budget and demanded the appointment of a committee to allocate expenditure between the spending departments. By the end of the session Balfour reluctantly appointed such a committee.

Churchill also protested at some terms of the Proclamation to end the Boer War because they threatened Boer leaders, who had not surrendered by the specified date. He had supported the war as a means of self-defence, but he thought its end should be procured with less. Further he opposed the demand of unconditional surrender, holding that, 'the British flag would be stripped of half its glory if it flew over a sullen and subjugated population, held down by the bayonets of a powerful army and a far-reaching system of police.'[3]

---

[1] Hansard, 13 May 1901.
[2] *Daily News* 14th May 1901.
[3] Chartwell Papers 2/18, 129.

Although I enjoyed the privilege of meeting in pleasant circumstances most of the Conservatives leaders, and was always treated with extraordinary kindness and good-nature by Mr Balfour; although I often saw Mr Chamberlain and heard him discuss affairs with the greatest freedom, I drifted steadily to the left. I found that Rosebery, Asquith, and Grey and above all John Morley seemed to understand my point of view far better than my own chiefs. I was fascinated by the intellectual stature of these men and their broad and inspiring outlook on public affairs, untrammelled as it was by the practical burden of events.[1]

---

[1] WSC, *My Early Life* ch. 29.

2

Free Trade
1903–4

Churchill showed his independence and strength of mind by opposing the Unionist inclination to protectionism. After some initial briefing from Sir Francis Mowatt at the Treasury, he mastered the argument himself. He became a believer in the concept of free trade which amounted to leaving trade free of government regulation, so that British people could buy and sell as they wished throughout the world. The opposite political belief was termed protection, under which government sought to regulate trade and commerce at the expense of individual freedom.

The repeal of the Corn Laws had restored free trade throughout the second half of the nineteenth century. Even the Tories, who traditionally embrace protection, had to uphold the new political regime of free trade; their group, the 'Free Fooders', comprised about sixty MPs, including Churchill and Lord Hugh Cecil. The engine of free trade in Parliament was the Liberal Party.

Churchill was inspired particularly by Richard Cobden, the leader of the free trade campaign of the 1840s. He paid tribute to him in Manchester on 19 February 1904:

> [I]t was Cobden's work to lay a mighty stone. I say it was Cobden's work not because he did it himself but somehow Cobden's name seemed to inherit the odium, and so he ought to have all the glory too. Other stones have been laid on the stone that Cobden laid; and even now there is plenty of work for the stonemasons and master builders. But we believe that the work which Cobden did was done forever; that the stone he laid shall never be translated; that the stone shall never been transplanted; that the heights he gained shall never be abandoned.[1]

The story of the Corn Laws in the 1840s was central to Churchill's understanding and, in order to understand his and the prevalent thinking in Parliament, it is useful to consider a brief outline of that campaign.

---

[1] Chartwell Papers 9/20/75.

The population in Britain had swelled from about 10 million in 1750 to about 25 million by 1815. Millions crowded into cities, particularly in the north. Grain had to be imported to feed about 3 million urban dwellers. The grain trade had attracted protection in various forms since a statute to regulate its export of 1436. Twenty years of war with France had encouraged domestic British production of grain. In 1815 Parliament, dominated by rural landowners, passed the Corn Laws, which prohibited imports of wheat below a price of 80/- per quarter. The Act was replaced in 1828 with a regime of sliding scales; the price at which wheat could be imported rose and fell in step with the home price up to a price of 72/- a quarter. But the margin between the two prices ensured a considerable premium for home producers over the international market and prevented the consumer enjoying both the foreign corn and the foreign trade which would pay for it.

During the 1830s businessmen began to realise that the Corn Laws operated to artificially increase the prices of food and so increase wages. In 1838, after an appalling harvest, a number of businessmen in the Lancashire cotton trade formed the Anti-Corn Law Association. They held meetings to explain the commercial case against the Corn Laws in Manchester and other industrial centres. In January 1839 the Association, later to be called the League, held a public dinner for 800. A fortnightly paper, the *Anti-Corn Law Circular*, was published in April 1839 and reached a circulation of 15,000 within six weeks. Although the northern towns were alive to the issue of the high price of corn, Lord Melbourne's government was deaf to the plight of the unemployed and to the distress of textile factory owners.

Cobden was returned as Member of Parliament for Stockport, Lancashire, in June 1841. He brought with him a keen sense of political principles, a sharper insight into the economic condition of the people than that held by the rural members. He was not deflected by stepping into public fame. The Commons did not make a show of their welcome; northern commercial men were resented as intruders. Cobden was seen as a troublemaker whom the Reform Act 1832 had brought into political life. His case was seen as specious sophistry. In September of that year he enlisted the active support of John Bright.

By the end of 1842, after four years of arguing for repeal, Sir Robert Peel, the Prime Minister, was coldly unsympathetic, Cobden was fatigued, trade was beginning to revive, the price of corn fell. Cobden and Bright took their cause during 1843 to rural towns and to the farmers. Yet, after their tour of England with meetings almost every week, the position of the Corn Laws still seemed secure; the weather was mild, the harvest reasonable, trade was reviving and the budget was balanced.

Nonetheless during this rural campaign Cobden had appreciated the agricultural dimension of the question more fully and began to realise that the Corn Laws operated only in favour of the rural landowners; tenant farmers gained nothing, for their rent rose commensurately with the price of corn, and the agricultural worker's earnings remained unaffected by artificially high prices of corn.. He distinguished between landowners and farmers. 'The landowner is no more an agriculturist than a ship-owner is a sailor,' he remarked with succinct sarcasm. He shocked the House with several speeches about the wretched condition of farm workers and tenant farmers. In particular, Cobden troubled the conscience of Peel by such examples as that the value of exports to Brazil in 1844 exceeded the annual consumption of goods by all the farm workers and their families in Britain.

The first weeks in August 1845 were cold and wet and a potato disease struck potatoes in the ground and in store. It was particularly severe in Ireland where the potato was the last resort in a diet that included neither meat nor corn. The only pis aller beneath a potato diet was starvation. The corn rotted in fields, unharvested, north of the Trent. The repeal of the Corn Laws had become inevitable. On 28 October Cobden attacked Peel before an audience of 8000 in Manchester; he would be a poltroon and a criminal, warned Cobden, if he did not open the ports to foreign wheat. As Cobden remarked, it was sad and ironic that an argument for abundance and plenty came upon its hour at a moment of dire distress.

The dire situation in Ireland forced the Conservative government to repeal the Corn Laws. It was a reform born of necessity, rather than conviction. However, Peel refused to lift them immediately. He repealed the Corn Laws gradually over three years. The measure was carried on the Third Reading by a majority of 98. Two thirds of his party voted against their leader. Within days the protectionists in the Tory Party, led by Disraeli, who had been stalking Peel for sometime, combined with the Whigs on the Irish Coercion Bill and voted Peel out of office.

The Anti-Corn Law League had fulfilled its object. There had been moments of success and intervals of dreary disappointment, but, finally, fortune had crowned their labours. The League was wound up. The Corn Laws were demolished over five years and Britain enjoyed free trade until the entry of Churchill into Parliament.

Returning to the opening of the twentieth century and to the situation confronting Churchill, free trade still held centre place on the political stage. But in the Budget of 1902 Sir Michael Hicks-Beach, hitherto a staunch free trader, imposed a registration duty on foreign grain. The duty was expected to yield £2.6 million in a full year. Churchill voted for this measure, but only as a wartime expedient. He was shaken by this departure from economic orthodoxy of the later half nineteenth century and he stated as much in the Commons. But he knew the Chancellor was really a staunch free trader and was aware of his friendship with his father.

Churchill swiftly grasped the free trade argument. Free trade was described by Sir Henry Campbell-Bannerman, the Liberal leader, as more like 'a law of gravitation', than a political argument. Churchill spoke on Budget day and warned of the danger of the 'fair trade' argument promoted, it was claimed to consolidate the Empire and to provide new revenue. Fair trade was just a different robe of protectionism.

On 14 November 1902 Churchill wrote to a constituent in terms which reveal his understanding of free trade:

> It [the British Empire] is very large [then comprising one quarter of the globe and amounting to 400 million people] and there are a good many things that can be produced in it, but the world is larger & produces some better things than can be found in the British Empire. Why should one deny ourselves the good and varied merchandise which the traffic of the world offers, more especially since we trade with others, the more they trade with us; for it is quite clear we give them something else back for everything they give us. Our planet is not a very big one compared with the other celestial bodies, and I see no particular reason why we should endeavour to make inside our planet a smaller planet called the British Empire, cut off by impassable space from everything else.[1]

And to another constituent in May 1903 he wrote, in the light of the large vision of free trade.

> I do not want a self-contained Empire. It is very much better that the great nations of the world should be interdependent one upon the other than that should be independent of each other. That makes powerfully for peace and it is chiefly through the cause of great traffic of one great nation with another during the last twenty five years, that the peace of Europe has been preserved through so many years.
>
> And if it comes to an European war, do you not think it very much better that the United States should be vitally interested in keeping the English market open, than they should be utterly careless of what happens to their principal customer?[2]

He attacked the protectionist stance of Pearson, who owned the *Evening Standard*, the *Daily Express* and several provincial newspapers. He concluded a letter to *The Times* thus: 'I would urge those who have influence upon public platforms to take every convenient occasion drawing attention to the developments which are now taking place, and, which so far as they are effective inevitable degrade journalism from the status of a humble profession like Medicine or Law to a sordid and irresponsible traffic in words and phrases.'

---

[1] R. Churchill, *Winston S. Churchill* vol. ii p. 53.
[2] Ibid. p. 57.

Churchill was a Member of young Tory back bench weekly dining club, called the 'Hooligans', or 'Hughligans,' after Lord Hugh Cecil, the younger son of the former Prime Minister, Lord Salisbury. This club was sometimes known also as the Malcolmtents, after Ian Malcolm. They shared dissatisfaction at the becalmed state of party politics. In May 1902 they invited Joseph Chamberlain to dinner. At that time he was the Colonial Secretary and better known in Parliament as the protectionist champion. As he was leaving at the end of the party he told his hosts: 'You young gentlemen have entertained me royally, and in return I give you a priceless secret. Tariffs! These are the politics of the future, and of the near future. Study them closely and make yourselves masters of them, and you will not regret your hospitality to me.'[1]

Churchill was ready to join the debate on free trade which had been established in Tory dogma since 1846. He wrote later, with the advantage of hindsight and the disadvantage of its complacency, '[W]hen the Protection issue was raised I was already disposed to view all their actions in the most critical light . . . Still I am sure that in those days I acted in accordance with my deepest feeling and with all that recklessness in so doing which belongs to youth and is indeed the glory of youth and its formidable quality.'[2]

Of Lord Hugh Cecil, then one of his closest friends, Churchill wrote: 'Here for the first time, and I am afraid almost for the last, I met a real Tory, a being out of the seventeenth century, but equipped with every modern convenience.'[3] Churchill worked with Cecil closely on the free trade issue. Cecil, or Linky, as Churchill called him, 'leapt into the political arena accoutred with every intellectual weapon and with earnest resolve to defend causes which nobody then seemed to consider very important and few people now bother about at all'.[4]

On 15 May 1903 Joe Chamberlain, the Colonial Secretary, opened his Tariff Reform campaign in Birmingham On that same day Balfour was trying to convince some farmers that the corn duties imposed earlier would have to be repealed. Chamberlain proposed to impose tariffs on trade outside the British Empire, in order to broaden the basis of tax, to reinforce the commercial cohesion of the Empire and to increase employment at home. An imperial tariff – a modest tax on food and 10% on manufactured goods – would, he ventured, increase imperial trade by £26 million per annum and that would provide employment for 166,000. He often referred to the menace of dumping by overseas producers. It has often been the stalking horse of protectionism. In September Chamberlain resigned as Colonial Secretary because he had no backing from the Prime Minister or Cabinet.

Chamberlain had been an ardent free trader and a rising radical in the Liberal

---

[1] WSC, *My Early Life* ch. 29.
[2] WSC *Thoughts and Adventures*, pp. 5–6.
[3] Ibid p. 36.
[4] Ibid.

Party during the early 1850s. In 1884 Lloyd George had predicted that Chamberlain would become a future leader of the people. Chamberlain had befriended Henry George, the American economist, and had been struck by his book *Progress and Poverty* in the early 1880s. After reading it, Chamberlain believed that the land question would be 'the great thing' in British politics. He had then disclosed an understanding of free trade. He spoke in the summer of 1881 against the 'reactionary and protectionist' commercial Treaty with France: 'A tax on food would raise the price of every article produced in the United Kingdom and would inevitably bring about a loss of that gigantic export trade.'[1] He had left the Liberal Party over the Irish question in 1886.

Yet in 1903 Chamberlain urged such a departure from nineteenth-century orthodoxy of free trade on two grounds: it would yield a new source of revenue and it would promote imperial unity by restricting trade outside the Empire. Churchill exposed this defence of protection for the purpose of raising revenue in the Commons in February 1904. 'Did the Rt. Hon. gentleman believe that the ugly rush to join the Tariff Commission proceeded from any exhalted enthusiasm for revenue: that those wealthy manufacturers sitting in conclave day after day and defraying their own expenses were there for the sole purpose of discovering a new source of revenue to balance the Budget for imperial purposes.'

Indeed the use of tariffs was one question and the raising of new revenue raised two further questions: what was the intended expenditure and what was the means of raising new revenue? In fact, it was intended to raise new revenue for social programmes, but only from those who were intended to be recipients of this state welfare and it would endeavour vainly to unite the empire, but at the cost of outlawing the rest of mankind. It was a mischievous policy; perhaps novel, popular but flawed in theory and in practical implementation. It was popular with the man in the street because they imagined that the tax would be paid by the foreigner: in fact, he, not the foreigner, would be paying. Tariff reform was popular with manufacturers who welcomed the slightest discouragement of their foreign competitors. But even though it appeared to be in their immediate interest, they ignored the fact that it would engulf trade with a mesh of corrupt and arbitrary controls.

Churchill liked him and respected his kindness but recognised the danger which his energy and ability posed to his party and nation and, indeed, to the world. He was determined to thwart his endeavours. If indeed patriotism is the last refuge of the scoundrel, then protectionism can be reckoned its handmaiden.

The Liberal Opposition were ranged against protectionism on grounds of economic strategy, principles of freedom and scruples of honesty. Campbell-Bannerman saw 'this reckless criminal escapade of Joe's as the great event of our time'. Chamberlain had afforded an opportunity to his Liberal opponents to

---

[1] J. Enoch Powell, *Joseph Chamberlain* p. 48.

13

parade their policy on free trade. Lloyd George, then rising in the Liberal Party, ridiculed tariff reform at Oldham in October 1903, '... when a statesman of Chamberlain's position comes forward and proposes a return to the old Corn Law days, lords and dukes and earls and squires and baronets are found running and clucking towards him like a flock of fowls when they hear corn shaken in the tin.'[1]

Churchill attacked tariff reform from the moment of its unveiling in public. It would have a destructive effect, he warned, on the Conservative Party. 'The old Conservative Party, which contained many protectionists with its religious convictions and constitutional principles will disappear and a new party will arise rigid, materialist and secular, whose opinions will turn on tariffs and who will cause the lobbies to be crowded with the touts of protected industries.'[2]

In the same month Churchill pointed to the essential advantages of free trade over protection in a letter published in *The Times*:

> I hold that, though free trade, like every other policy, has its defects in this imperfect world, still on the whole the abundance of commodities, the simplicity of our Customs arrangements, the freedom of our ports, the adaptiveness of our industries, the purity of our public life give to our workers much more than foreign nations are able to gain by tariff jiggles, usually stupid, often corrupt.

The following month he shared a platform with Lord Hugh Cecil in the Town Hall, Birmingham, which was the headquarters of the Chamberlains. The meeting passed off without the expected disorders. Churchill regretted that he did not spot many old friends; 'But it is part of the price a politician has to pay if he refuses to jump with the jumping cat.'[3]

Churchill had earlier gave vent to his frustration in a letter to *The Times*:

> The greatest question of the day may be argued in the Palace and in the coal-hole. Every chamber of commerce may debate it. Every public body may pass a resolution. It is on the agenda of the Eton Political Society. It is in the Parliament of Peckham. But there is one place where it is "taboo". The House of Commons, most interested, most concerned, most respectable, is to be gagged and smothered by a cynical and inglorious abuse of its own procedures.[4]

In August 1903 Chamberlain wrote to Churchill to advise him that there was 'not much room in politics for a dissident Tory in politics, but Heaven knows that

---

[1] E. T. Raymond, *Lloyd George* p. 90.
[2] *Hansard*, 22 June 1903.
[3] *Daily News*. 12 Nov 1903.
[4] *Times* 16 July 1903.

the other side stands most in need new talent, and I expect you will drift there before long'.[1] In the autumn of 1903 the Tory Party in Oldham first manifested their unease with the opinions of their Member. In November the Conservative Club in North Chadderford was barred against him. The Press demanded a statement. Churchill told them, 'I am in favour of Free Trade and Free Speech.'[2] In December the General Purposes Committee withdrew their willingness to provide their services at the next election to Churchill. Churchill confided to Hugh Cecil that 'I am an English Liberal. I hate the Tory party, their men, their words & their methods.'[3]

In November 1903 Churchill spoke in the Commons about the issue:

> Thank God for the Liberal party. But, after all, it was with the Liberal party that the main conduct of this great struggle must rest. English Liberalism had been through many years of wanderings and of tribulation, and had arrayed against it today immense forces of authority and interest and yet they knew that it was still a massive instrument which, in the hands of Mr Gladstone or of old John Bright, would easily smash into pieces the music-hall Imperialism and pantomime finance by which they were plagued.

Churchill had reached the conclusion that protectionism promoted under the slogan tariff reform must be halted. On 22 December he wrote to a correspondent, 'you may be perfectly safe that in following the Duke of Devonshire [a free trader] you will run no risk of being committed to such wild and dangerous schemes as may easily result from Mr Chamberlain's violence or Mr Balfour's weakness, or worst of all, from a combination of them both.'[4]

Churchill wrote to the Liberal candidate in Ludlow, Mr Horne, a free trader, wishing him luck against his Conservative opponent, a protectionist.

> The system of free trade involves conditions of profound importance to those whose votes you are seeking – cheap food & honest Government. Mr Chamberlain's victory would deprive us of both . . . All these years we have held up among the monopolies and all kinds of corruption, millions of Free-traders in America and Germany are struggling forward by various roads towards that liberty and justice which we have long enjoyed. We must not extinguish our beacon just when its light is most needed. All these years the good of England has meant the welfare of the world . . .

---

[1] *Chartwell Papers* 2/8 57.
[2] *Manchester Guardian*, 20 Nov 1903.
[3] R. Churchill, *Winston S. Churchill* vol ii p. 71.
[4] Chartwell Papers 2/10 34.

The triumph of Protection would set up instead a policy of brag and grab.[1]

When protection is embraced politicians are afforded a discretion in conferring monopolies and, invariably, this discretion leads them, in reality, to seek popularity and, in pretence, to inventing fake national interests. As Churchill encapsulated the essence of the free trade principle: 'Justice to all – Preference to none!'

---

[1] R. Churchill. *Winston S. Churchill* vol ii, Companion Pt. i p. 266–7.

3

Free Thinker
1904–6

The Unionist government was led from 1902 by a master strategist, Balfour. He had succeeded his uncle in July as the Prime Minister. He had come into what Churchill called 'an exhausted inheritance'. His manoeuvring was not impeded in any direction by anything as fixed and inconvenient as a principle. He was an intellectual. He studied philosophy, logic and scientific research, particularly in chemistry. He read literature and poetry widely. He also devoured detective stories and French light literature. In music he liked Handel, Bach and Wagner.

He had a dry wit, but often a politician's wit does not read as vividly as it was first heard. Yet Balfour was seemingly an exception. In the Commons he said of another speaker, 'In that oration there were some things that were true, and some things that were trite; but what was true was trite, and what was not trite was not true.' Or again, 'There were some things in it meant seriously, which were humorous, and that there were others meant humorously which were serious.'[1]

He was a friend even to his political opponents. Churchill enjoyed his conversation. He was wealthy and untroubled either by the bustle of life or the finality of death. He remained a bachelor. He never read newspapers. Churchill and others tried to convince him of the need to glean useful bits of information by adopting the habit. 'I have never put myself', he replied to them,' to the trouble of rummaging an immense rubbish heap on the problematic chance of discovering a cigar end.'[2] He was a noted expert on defence. In politics he appeared often ill at ease. He was too clever to enjoy any rapport with a public, who expected a more earthy leader – a womaniser, horse lover, drinker, gambler, even a hero or clown – whom they could comprehend.

Politics requires a distinct type of intelligence, to discern true principles from party dogma of a type that draws forth those inane, prolonged sighs of approval from the back benches; politics requires courage and character of a type that can be learnt and seldom taught; it demands a breadth of vision that extends far

---

[1] WSC, *Great Contemporaries* p. 158.
[2] Ibid p. 159.

beyond personal popularity, in order to encompass the need of man for freedom. Balfour was intelligent and witty but he was not in the mould of a statesman.

Ian Malcolm, a Tory backbencher, recalled his first glimpse of Balfour on his feet in the House. 'Did I say thousands?', Balfour questioned while himself answering a interjection. Then calmly, to our consternation, 'Oh, I meant millions, but it makes no difference to my argument.'[1]

Balfour was neither a free trader nor a protectionist. He defined his position with disingenuous imprecision in a letter to Churchill, who had written to him about his worries of Chamberlain's new protectionist policy in May 1903.

> I have never understood that Chamberlain advocated protection, though no doubt, he is ready and, indeed, anxious – for a duty on foodstuffs, which may incidentally be protective in its character, but whose main object is to provide an instrument of fiscal union with the Colonies. That is a very different thing from protection, both in theory and in practice. But undoubtedly the matter is one of extreme difficulty, and requires the most wary walking.[2]

Churchill referred him thereafter as 'a great Free Trader out of school-hours.'[3]

Balfour had pledged, when succeeding Lord Salisbury as Tory leader in 1902, to make no change in party policy. He preferred to continue without being drawn into either camp. He had forced out his Chancellor of the Exchequer, Charles Ritchie, who was a steadfast free trader, because he threatened to split the party. Balfour shed him simply by denying him support in Cabinet. 'He had the manners of a pirate and the courage of a governess,' remarked Balfour, who remained quite unmoved by his departure. In September 1903 Chamberlain resigned as Secretary of the Colonies in Cabinet. Balfour allowed Ritchie and Lord Balfour, both free traders in the Cabinet, to go without informing them that Chamberlain, whose presence in the cabinet caused their decision, had also tendered his resignation. The Duke of Devonshire, another free trader, resigned without realising Chamberlain had already gone. Balfour had freed himself from both sides in this struggle. He regarded them as a governess might regard children fighting over some childish issue. He described the debate between free traders and protectionists as a mere 'squabble'. Yet he filled the two vacancies in Cabinet with dedicated protectionists: Austen Chamberlain, the son of Joe Chamberlain became Chancellor and Alfred Lyttelton became Colonial Secretary. Churchill thought Balfour was 'careful to shed Free Trade and Protectionist blood as far as possible in equal quantities. Like Henry V111, he decapitated Papists and hot

---

[1] I. Malcolm, *Balfour* p. 23.
[2] K. Young, *Arthur James Balfour* p. 212.
[3] V. Bonham Carter, *Churchill As I Knew Him* p. 101.

Gospellers on the same day for their respective divergences from his central, personal and artificial compromise.'[1] 'Here is a Cabinet shattered, split – and yet it lives. It is like a worm cut in twain , but both ends wiggle – blindly,' observed Lloyd George.[2]

Churchill sought to force Balfour to speak about the split which Chamberlain had opened between free traders and protectionists in the Unionist Party. He knew he had an unanswerable case but any opportunity to deploy it was denied him by his leader. He became a thorn in the side of his leader's suave intellectual approach to administration. Balfour carefully was absent from the House of Commons whenever Churchill was speaking. He felt the fragility of his position and admitted on 10 June in the House that, 'I should consider I was but ill performing my duty if I were to profess a settled conviction when no settled conviction exists'.[3] Indeed he was speaking the truth: his party was hopelessly divided. To suggest Balfour was timid would be unfair. He was trying to hold the Unionist Party together. He could not compete in protectionist demagogery with Chamberlain. He regarded Sir Robert Peel as an unpardonable poltroon for having split the Unionist Party in 1846. Though that split had been over the repeal of the Corn Laws, which marked the introduction of free trade, it did not diminish his treachery in Balfour's mind. He was interested in party unity above anything else.

Lloyd George could not restrain his delight at the Tory disarray and the reluctance of the Prime Minister to show decision and leadership. At Newcastle Lloyd George said in April 1903, 'There is too much disposition to tune our lyre to the sounds that come from the street, instead of from the good old principles of Liberalism. Who is the man in the street? . . . [He] is the man who gives neither time nor any serious thought to the study of politics. [A voice: Balfour] No, he is the man on the golf links.'

In January 1904 the Tories censured Churchill for uttering 'scurrilous statements against His Majesty Edward VII'. But Churchill replied, 'This appears to me to be utter nonsense; and I challenge the members of your committee to produce the slightest shadow of foundation in any speech of mine for such a ridiculous and abominable charge.' The local party decided to stand by him. In the House of Commons he moved to a seat below the gangway in token of his rebellion against the inclination of the Unionist Party towards protectionism.

On 22 January it was reported in the *Daily Telegraph* that the Tory whip had been withdrawn from Churchill and other free traders in the party. Churchill complained to Balfour that this should be reported to a newspaper before he had been informed. Balfour apologised and reinstated the whip, pleading he had been led to such a step by Churchill's recent public statements.

Speaking at the inaugural meeting of the Free Trade League on 19 February at

---

[1] WSC, *World Crisis* 1911–14 pp. 28–9.
[2] P. Rowland, *lloyd George* p. 173.
[3] House of Commons, 10 June 1903.

Manchester, Churchill showed how far he had moved towards the Liberal Party, for whom free trade was an article of faith.

> We contend that for a nation to tax itself into prosperity is like a man standing in a bucket and trying to lift himself up by the handle. But if the theory be true, what a curious position we should be in. What a mistake it would have been to build the Manchester Ship Canal. Here is a great work, built what for? To facilitate dumping – to pour a stream of foreign imports into the heart of industrial Britain . . . .
>
> The British Empire is held together by moral not by material forces. It has grown up in liberty and silence. It is not preserved by restriction and vulgar brag.[1]

The Tories punished Churchill for what they saw as his treachery by leaving the chamber as soon as Balfour rose to speak. As a party they were not only abandoning their policy on free trade, of which Chamberlain had twenty years before been an ardent champion, but they were betraying the national interest in the maintenance of commercial freedom, as it had been enjoyed since 1846.

Finally, on 31 May 1904 Churchill entered the House, paused at the Bar and then took a seat next to Lloyd George on the Liberal benches: he had crossed the floor from the Conservative to the Liberal benches. He occupied the corner seat below the Opposition gangway, from which his father had shelled Gladstone so vehemently. The layout of the House made crossing to the Opposition an especially decisive move. While it was possible to move from one gradient to another without attracting too much notice, crossing the floor was a different manoeuvre altogether. In case it was supposed the move was a casual mistake, he repeated the manoeuvre in the same day again.

Churchill was detested for this move. It was seen as betrayal to Unionists; not just to their party but to the Flag, Crown and Nation; to the veritable totems of Toryism. It was a brave and characteristic move. From that moment he began a partnership in political matters with Lloyd George. In the smoking room of the Commons, a lively cockpit of gossip, members thought he had made a mistake. Principles were reckoned as pitfalls and generally, as obstacles to advancement.

In the election campaign of 1906 he was accused of opportunism and he replied, 'Some men change their Party for the sake of their principles; others change their principles for the sake of their Party.' Any notion that Churchill had grasped the convenient issue of free trade is misconceived. Originally he had believed it was the tradition of his party, but gradually he perceived that principles rather than party formed the exciting ground of politics. Ideas and

---

[1] Chartwell Papers 9/20, 72.

thinking distinguish individuals from each other. Conformity denotes packs and parties.

He retained the close friendship of some Tory colleagues on a social level – Balfour himself, Lord Hugh Cecil and F.E. Smith, with whom he was to form an especially close friendship. Even Chamberlain confided with him, 'I think you are quite right, feeling as you do, to join the Liberals.'[1]

Churchill felt for the individual who was oppressed by the whipped and unthinking phalanxes of vested interests which dominate the House, as he disclosed to the Annual Dinner of the Liverpool Philharmonic Society in 1904:

> The private Member, we are told, is a public nuisance. Poor wretch! He gets in the way of combinations. He has to go under too. He is the small trader when the big combine comes along. The independent Member – the Member on whom the Whips cannot quite rely to hold his tongue and vote straight – no words are bad enough for him.
>
> I believe in personality. The House of Commons depends for its popularity, and consequently for its power, on the personality of its members. How shall art live without personality, without men who will back their own conception against the world? Without, let us say, the painter who will declare 'it is this thus that pictures should be painted. It is thus that immaculate motherhood, or surprise, or anger or hope should be portrayed; it may not be after this school or that, but it is as I see it.' Without the sculptor who labours after his own ideal striving to show in unsympathetic stone what he thinks is the shape of beauty. Without the poet, disdainful of public opinion, writing gloomily for himself.[2]

Churchill spent a lot of time advancing the free trade argument in the country. In May 1904, while sharing a platform with, he described the Unionist Party:

> We know perfectly well what to expect – a party of great vested interests, banded together in a formidable confederation, corruption at home, aggression to cover it up abroad, the trickery of tariff jiggles, the tyranny of a party machine; sentiment by the bucketful, patriotism by the imperial pint, the open hand at the public exchequer, the open door of the public house, dear food for the million, cheap labour for the millionaire. That is the policy of Birmingham and we are going to erect against the policy of Birmingham the policy of Manchester.[3]

He went to warn that the next election there would be a substantial question to

---

[1] W.S.C, *Great Contemporaries*, p. 44.
[2] Chartwell Papers 9/13, 41-6.
[3] *Manchester Guardian*, 14 May 1904.

be determined. 'All through this winter we have listened to a revival of the stale, old, exploded Protection; to all sorts of doctrines and theories about trade and commerce which it had been hoped in the twentieth century we had cast behind us as the ancient popular beliefs in magic and witchcraft.'[1]

Speaking at Alexandra Palace, London, in June 1904 Churchill took a typically broad view of the issue.

> Men change, manners change, customs change, Governments and Prime Ministers change, even Colonial Secretaries [Chamberlain was that Secretary] – sometimes they change their offices, sometimes they change their opinions. But principles do not change. Whatever was scientifically true in the economic propositions which were established sixty years ago in a far greater generation than our own is just as true in 1904 as it was in 1846, and it will still be true as long so long as men remain trading animals on the habitable globe.

In November he wrote to Lord Salisbury who had questioned the severity of his attacks on the leadership of his former party. Churchill's reply evidences his spirit.

> I readily admit that his conduct is open to criticism, not – thank heaven – on the score of sincerity, but from the point of view of taste . . . I had to choose between fighting & standing aside. No doubt the latter was the more decorous. But I wanted to fight – I felt I could fight with my whole heart and soul.[2]

'The House of Commons', Churchill reminded himself, 'is a jealous mistress: you must give her the cream of your thought.' He spoke in Commons on 8 March 1905:

> I have been told that within thirty miles of the Manchester Exchange – I might say of the Free Trade Hall – there is gathered together the greatest concentration of human beings on the surface of the globe. This mass of people are absolutely dependent . . . on the condition of a crop at one end of the world, and the state of the market at the other; and yet, upon this artificial foundation, through the estimable advantages of unfettered enterprise, and of unrestricted sea communication, they have been able to build up a vast industrial fabric, which, it is no exaggeration to say, is the economic marvel of the world . . . With the telegraph and the steamships there is hardly a food-exporting country in the word that is

---

[1] Ibid.
[2] R. Churchill, *Winston S. Churchill* vol ii p. 93.

more than sixty days from Liverpool. The harvests of the world at our disposal, and, by a system which averages climatic risks, we secure not merely a low but a fairly stable price. With that marvellous operation by which the crowded operation of this isle is fed, we cannot take the responsibility of interfering. There will be good years and there will bad years. Great fluctuations must necessarily occur from time to time in all commodities which depend on climatic conditions ... There are many factors in price – harvests, freight, speculations – which do not recognise the House of Commons. Taxes alone remain in our hands ... Quite apart from the economic argument, we do no want to see the British Empire degenerate into a sullen confederacy, walled off, like a mediaeval town, from the surrounding country; victualled for a siege, and containing within the circle of its battlements all that is necessary for war. We want this country and the States associated with it to take their parts freely and fairly in the general intercourse of commercial nations. We do not mind even if we become dependent on foreign nations, because we know that by that very fact we make foreign nations dependent on us.[1]

Churchill attempted to confront Balfour on free trade in the Commons. In January 1905 he attacked him in Manchester, saying:

I am not surprised that Mr Balfour has declared that he does not intend to dissolve Parliament. Abdications have taken place in the history of the world ... Kings have abdicated but never Queens, and it one of the attractive qualities that his nature displays, a certain femininity.[2]

But this fugitive leader either was absent from the Chamber or he left hurriedly as Churchill rose to speak. Once in the autumn of 1905 Churchill attacked the absent Balfour. It was just, therefore, that Churchill should play a leading role in the downfall of his former leader. In March 1905 a Private Member's motion, censured 'the Prime Minister's policy of Fiscal Retaliation'. Churchill rose to ask where the Prime Minister had been during the debate of this Resolution. 'To keep in office for a few more weeks and months there is no principle which the Government are not prepared to abandon, no friend or colleague they are not prepared to betray, and no quantity of dust and filth they are not prepared to eat.'[3] On the following day Churchill asked Balfour if the Resolution was to be expunged. The Prime Minister said he was unaware of it, until Churchill had drawn his attention to it. Then he read it and affected complete disinterest in it. It did not seem to him to require any particular move on his part.

---

[1] Hansard vol 141 col 810–13.
[2] *Times* 29 January 1905..
[3] Hansard, 28 March 1905.

The Conservative government suffered a further defeat in the Commons during July. But Balfour survived without sign of distress and preserved a facade of unity held together, said Churchill, by 'a succession of formulas designed to enable people who differed profoundly, to persuade themselves that they were in agreement.'[1] At the end of July Churchill told the House of Commons of his party's frustration.

Balfour replied the same day to rebuke his young assailant for lack of taste. 'It is not on the whole', advised Balfour, 'desirable to come down to the House with invective which is prepared and violent ... If there is preparation there is more finish and if there is so much violence there should be more vivacity of feeling'. Churchill accepted the rebuke in good spirit and conceded that the Prime Minister had made a good speech.

In September 1905 Churchill wrote to Henry Gladstone, a Liberal Shadow Minister, pleading exhaustion. He reckoned that he had held more than fifty meetings in the previous twelve months. In April of the previous year he had lost his way during a speech in the House of Commons. Everyone feared that he had broken down or that he had not prepared his speech sufficiently. He never developed the gift of speaking spontaneously while making speeches. He needed rest.

Lloyd George, fearing that Balfour would postpone a General Election until 1906, remarked 'They will die with their drawn salaries in their hands.'[2] Balfour called for unity at the annual conference of the National Unionists in November at Newcastle. Chamberlain ignored his leader by demanding a general election in which the Unionist Party could issue a strong policy on tariff reform. That decision had forced Balfour's hand. On 4 December 1905 Balfour resigned. He resigned personally as Prime Minister and Conservative leader and the Conservative Government resigned as well. There had been no defeat in the Commons. No Prime Minister has tendered his own and his party's resignation without such a defeat since.

Churchill was appointed Under-Secretary for the Colonies in the Liberal Government of Sir Henry Campbell-Bannerman on 13 December. He turned down the offer of Financial Secretary at the Treasury in order to have the opportunity of leading in the House of Commons, as his Secretary of State, Lord Elgin, was in the House of Lords. Churchill described the ninth Earl of Elgin as 'a rugged old Thane of antique virtue and simplicity'. Besides the advantage of becoming a front- bench spokesman in the Commons on a subject dominated by affairs in South Africa, the office had been held by Sunny, the Duke of Marlborough, his cousin and that counted with Churchill.[3] It was not a grand position, Cecil dismissed it as a 'stipendiary echo', but it was a start.

---

[1] WSC, *The World Crisis* vol i p. 28.
[2] Sir Almeric Fitzroy, *Memoirs* vol i p. 266.
[3] V. Bonham Carter, *Churchill As I Knew Him* p. 146.

One of Churchill's first acts as a Minister was to appoint Edward Marsh, a bright young civil servant in the Colonial Office, as his Private Secretary. When offered the post Marsh recalled that he 'betook myself to Lady Lytton, who was a great friend of his [Churchill] as well as mine, and poured out my misgivings. Her answer was one of the nicest that could have been said about anybody: 'The first time you meet Winston you see all his faults, and the rest of your life you spend in discovering his virtues; and so it proved.'[1] Marsh served Churchill in several ministries for thirty years. He was interested in literature and became Editor of *Georgian Poetry*. He was also the patron of young poets among whom was included Rupert Brooke.

---

[1] R. Churchill, *Winston S. Churchill* p. 111.

4

Property and Taxation

Free trade was the idea which attracted Churchill to the Liberal Party. Once he had joined them, he embraced their policy of the taxation of value of land. He became aware that both policies operated together to cut through economic injustice. Free trade cut out a great deal of unnecessary bureaucracy and focused the attention of the people and their government on a form of taxation which secured a just distribution of wealth. The taxation of the value of land proved to be the last stand of radical liberalism in British political life. It was a cause which Churchill took up with enthusiasm and to which he gave passionate and eloquent expression. His speeches on the subject of land value rank among the most memorable uttered on economic subjects from a British minister.

A basic political question concerns the precise meaning of the word property. In ordinary usage property means something owned, such as a piece of land, house, anything made by man. In this form it is too imprecise. In its legal sense property means, not the thing itself, but the right to it. That it is the sense in which it is used.

In politics an essential distinction has to be made between private property and public property. It is not enough to leave it for Parliament to determine as its majority is wont to do. For at various times an undertaking is considered private and at another public and vice versa. Assuredly, fundamental meanings and concepts are the pillars of political thought. Just as there cannot be language without common agreement about the meaning of words, or arithmetic without agreement about the value of figures, there cannot be political thought without removing key definitions from politics altogether.

It has been said that parliament can do anything it wishes, but it was remarked that it lacked the ability to make a man a woman or the colour black white. Such things are determined by nature. Parliament has sovereignty over British law but none over nature. By law it cannot undo the distinctions arising from the nature of Creation or alter its intelligence or subtleties. Mankind was not spilled haphazardly onto earth, like pieces in a giant jig-saw, and bidden to fight amongst itself for survival.

Certain gifts were bestowed on man in order to make life possible to sustain.

Air, sunshine, water and land can be considered as gifts to mankind in common. Plainly, rights, or property in these gifts, cannot be vested in certain individuals. In order to appropriate air an individual has only to breathe, or to enjoy sunshine move into its beam. Water can be appropriated merely by being collected in a private vessel. Can land be privately appropriated? Certainly its produce can be. A wild berry can be converted from a gift of nature into private property by being picked. But land, being a common gift, cannot be considered as subject matter to which property, either private or public, can be attached. The four gifts of nature share basic attributes. None is made by man and each is necessary for human life. No human legislative can declare otherwise, without making a fool of itself.

Property necessarily arises from human creation. In the remote regions of earth, where there are no conditions conducive to human life, the gift of nature is apparent. Yet the distinction between public and private property has to be found in bustling centres of life.

The hallmark of property is that it can attach only to things made by man. Public property attaches to things made by societies and private property to things made by individuals or bodies of individuals. Plainly something produced by a single craftsman afford the simplest example of the latter. The maker of a table possesses the best property in it. He can give that title away or leave it to his heirs or he can sell his title to a purchaser or he can abandon the chair. Legally the question of property in articles stolen, abandoned or appropriated usually creates a picnic for lawyers, but such matters would only be digressions from the main distinction between private and public property. The basic principle about private property is that it rests with whomever can trace title back to the maker of that thing.

Public property is simple to distinguish. It attaches to things created equally by mankind. Plainly it cannot be attached to the four gifts of nature. For they were made by the power that created man himself. It would be ridiculous for parliament to claim the sky over Britain as public property of the British.

Of the four natural elements the concept of property has been attached most often to land. It remains throughout the duration of the Universe the property of the maker of man. Occasionally a claim is made that certain pieces of land have been manufactured by human effort. Dykes may exclude the sea from areas of land, rubbish might be tipped until a surface emerges above the water or uninhabitable terrain may be drained. Property attaches in such cases not to land but to the dykes, mounds and drains created by human work.

However, land acquires a value according to human demand for its use. Within the Arctic Circle or in a desert where there is no substantial demand and, therefore, no value. But in a large capital city land value reflects the greater demand, whereas in a remote village its lower values evidence of lower demand. The value of land is indeed created by man and can be, therefore, the subject matter of property. Given that demand does not create value when only one individual desires the same land, plainly this value of land is not an individual creation. Public demand cannot be apportioned in varying degrees to individuals. The demand for land arises from the babe in arms. A falling birthrate will be reflected in a short time in the declining value of land. As every newcomer to earth arrives with this birthright of sharing in the value which their arrival enhanced or maintained, so the value belongs to everyone equally and to nobody in particular. The value of land is thus public property. So also are things created at public expense like public buildings and their contents and such things as language. But unlike these the value of land constitutes a profitable resource for use by a society.

Nature, as it affects man rather than animals, is a source of generosity and abundance. It has provided to an individual private property in everything the individual produces and to a society public property in the value which it creates.

It is supreme human wisdom to conform to nature. She has created no wars, famines, plagues, poverty or enslavement. Unhappily these are solely the bitter fruits of man's ignorance and injustice. Throughout the Western world governments impose tax on private property and allow public property to be appropriated as private property. The determination of property is a political matter. In Britain the law is concerned only with the quiet possession of land. Parliament awards property in land value by failing to impose taxation upon it.

English law is concerned with the quiet possession of land. Clearly quiet possession is a a fundamental natural right of every individual. A community cannot sit at the same table, sleep in the same bedroom or sit in the same study. In order to create private property in quiet possession of land and things upon it, the individual or body of individuals who wish to possess it, must compensate those who have to be necessarily excluded from it.

The private ownership of land value necessarily results in the greater number of a society be dispossessed of their birthright and having to live in a landless condition. The private ownership of land value is a political creation. Parliament over centuries have sanctioned the freehold estate in land in plain contradiction of nature. They have allowed individuals to appropriate public property as their private property. In so doing, they have allowed society to be deranged from its natural course. From the confusion of private and public property has resulted the fact that in Britain, as elsewhere, private property, arising from individual labour which should be inviolate from public taxation, has become public property and the value of land, naturally valuable public property, has been allowed to become become private property.

John Locke wrote that the supreme duties of government were to protect civil liberty and individual property. He discountenanced the idea that men derived their rights from human laws and declared that the important rights the right to civil liberty and to private property were implanted in man by nature, whose order was finer and more intelligent than the systems devised by man. His basic argument was taken up by the French statesman Turgot,who pursued the argument with scholarship and integrity.

In an essay written in 1766 and published in 1769-70, entitled *Réflexions sur la formation et la distribution des richesses*, Turgot set out the basic principles of his political thought. When land was available, he asserted, the level of earnings was the amount an individual could produce on marginal land, or the least productive land in use. When, however, land was fully enclosed, earnings were fixed by competition between landless folk. Their competition drove the level of earnings down to the level of bare subsistence.

He also demonstrated that taxation should be levied on the *produit net*, or surplus accruing from production on superior land. Turgot was derided by nineteenth-century economists for having formulated his 'iron law of wages'. What he had revealed, however, was the plight of landless individuals. Not only were they required to compete among themselves for work but they were unjustly burdened with taxation levied on their earnings. Later he showed how disastrous it was to levy taxes on production. On superior land giving rise to a surplus, the taxes could be shifted onto the *produit net*, but on marginal land, on which there was no surplus, the burden of taxation could not be shifted. Turgot estimated that four-sevenths of France was marginal. There taxation on production gave rise not only to harassment of poor tenants but also to widespread unemployment.

In his essay Turgot also showed that the *produit net*, or the natural surplus, of superior land, was available for taxation. Indeed, he showed that it could be taxed without causing any derangement to the economy. In short, the *produit net* was a naturally public property: it was created by and, therefore, belonged to the community.

Turgot sought to apply his thinking both to draw France back from the brink of revolution and to transform herself into a great example to mankind. He was hounded from office by the resolute opposition of those with interests and privileges to protect.

In 1776 Adam Smith published his book *The Wealth of Nations*. The acclamation which greeted this work obscured Turgot's work on the Continent and in Britain. Turgot's thinking, however, emerged again in the late nineteenth century and caught the attention of John Morley, later a Liberal statesman, who befriended Churchill soon after he arrived in Parliament. He wrote at the end of a 120-page essay on Turgot, '. . . the keyword to Turgot's political aims and social theory was not Pity or Benevolence but Justice. It was justice also, not temporary Prejudice or Passion, that guided his judgment through the heated issues of the time. This justice and exact reasonableness it was impossible to surprise or throw of its guard'.[1] Morley had a wide knowledge of history and literature. Yet he said, 'If I know the work and character of any man in history, 'tis Turgot.'[2] To Morley, Turgot was the model of the philosopher statesman.

---

[1] J. Morley, *Critical Miscellanies*, vol. 11 pp. 160–1.
[2] F. W. Knickerbocker, *John Morley and his Friends* p. 138.

The Wealth of Nations gave birth to the study of economics on loose and complex foundations. The work began somewhere in the middle of the subject and reached, despite its length, no fixed principles of justice on such important matters as taxation; and terminated as unsatisfactorily as it had begun. It inspired Ricardo and John Stuart Mill and others to add little to Smith's thinking on taxation.

Cobden spent his public life promoting free trade. But he was aware that the taxation of land values was a fundamental and just reform, as he spoke at Derby on 10 December 1841: 'I hope to see societies formed calling upon the Legislature to revalue land and put taxation upon it in proportion to the wants of the State.'[1] He realised that free trade and taxation were necessary for a people to hold politicians within democratic disciplines.

Similar ideas to Turgot were promulgated independently by Henry George, a journalist in California, who at first had no knowledge of Turgot. George was a man without advantages of scholarship or a position in public life. Indeed he was harried by poverty, which fastened his mind keenly on the question of how it was that the progress of society, which he saw happening in California, seemed to be accompanied inexorably by poverty. He saw that communities created land value as a natural fund for taxation and that all man-made things should be exempt from taxation. He observed settlement in the developing savannah in the west of North America. All went well in a growing community as long as settlers could work on free land. Earnings rose to what a man or woman could earn by themselves on their own land. But once land was fully enclosed a less beneficial process occurred. New arrivals had to seek work in competition with each other from landlords. Earnings fell to the least that a man would accept and that depended on the state of competition between those seeking work. A pool of unemployed dragged the level of earnings to the minimum that an unemployed man would demand.

This was the same conclusion reached by Turgot, though George's work was more developed, since he lived after the industrial revolution, of which the beginnings only were evident in Turgot's time. As the community grew so there emerged landowners who happened to have enclosed sites which were to become valuable as, say, a main street, a station or a dock. They were few when compared with the increasing number looking for work. No landlord has ever earned his riches from land value; the community had done that for him. In every corner of the globe it is the same process. What is being claimed by private individuals was created by others. George reiterated that he was attacking a system of the private appropriation of land value due to public ignorance; he had no particular malevolence towards private landowners.

In his book *Progress and Poverty*, which appeared in 1879, George set out his

---

[1] *A Penny Tax on Land Values*: articles in *The Daily Chronicle* Nov 1908–Feb 1909 p. 19.

explanation of the creation of communal and of individual wealth and also his remedy: the taxation of land value. Just as society created this value, so it was perfectly lawful and natural, he argued, for it to recover what it had sown. He did not talk of land nationalisation or ownership of land by the state.

He showed that if an individual required a piece of land on which to build his house or on which to work in country or city, he was bound to pay the community for his quiet possession of land the annual value of the land, from which he necessarily excluded others. This payment reflected only its bare site value without any regard to the value of human improvements or buildings on the land. He was acknowledging a higher law of nature which ordained a perfect division into public and private property. Every individual has precisely the same claim to land value; it is their birthright. Being a monarch or a rich and powerful magnate did not entitle an individual to any greater right than that right enjoyed by the poorest in the land. That right is honoured if an individual requiring possession of land pays those, being the rest of the community, who are effectively displaced by his possession. George was making a clear distinction between the value of land and the value of improvements on it or, in other words, between the provision of nature and the works of man.

Turgot and George were at one in demonstrating two consequences of governing a state with no regard to universal realities. They saw in essence that when states were governed in accordance with nature's laws, they would succeed in much the same way that, for example, an aeroplane, which was built in accordance with the laws of aerodynamics, would fly. If nature was not obeyed, the consequences would be dire in both cases.

The first consequence, inflation, and, second, unemployment would become endemic. Inflation is caused, they showed, by the constant increase of taxes laid on private property. For in a society, in which land is fully enclosed, earnings are reduced to the least the landless will accept in real terms; earnings are valued in terms of what they buy. A tax on incomes or goods reduces the real value of earnings. Such a tax causes a rise in nominal earnings, as people attempt to restore the value of their earnings. The increase of earnings promotes a rise in prices, which has the twin effect of reducing earnings and government revenue. In this constant shifting of tax, government is at war continually with worker and entrepreneur, who pass taxation onto each other in the form of higher prices. Inflation acts as the safety valve to release the pressure. Inflation is the release mechanism for a society oppressed by taxation. Without it there would be deadlock.

Unemployment was a second consequence of taxation of private property. First, land enclosure denied the mass of mankind any right to earn the full product of their labour. So taxation was levied on earnings – whether indirectly on goods or by direct taxes on persons. Furthermore, taxation could be shifted on to landowners holding land of better quality yielding a surplus or rent. But much production took place on marginal land of little or no value, which did not yield a surplus, and so taxes could not be shifted onto landowners. Marginal land, by definition, does not yield more than earnings. Thus taxation of production on marginal land would be deducted from earnings and drive the margin out of production. In short, land enclosure had the twin disadvantage of depriving men of the chance to work for themselves and it deprived the community of land value which it had created. Taxation levied on production laid the foundation for inflation, unemployment and poverty.

Henry George became famous throughout the world. He visited Britain three times between 1882–90 and his work was acclaimed in Scotland, particularly in Glasgow. In London during his visit of 1881–2 he met Herbert Spencer, the philosopher. George had always admired the unambiguous writing in his book, *Social Statics*, on the inequity of private ownership of land. Yet he found him a cold, conceited fellow. Later, after the philosopher had disclaimed his earlier views, which John Morley had raised in an article, George wrote a book, *The Perplexed Philosopher*, to expose Spencer's cowardice and dishonesty.

George's ideas took hold in Scotland and particularly in the field of local government. In 1895, within fourteen years of his first visit the Corporation of Glasgow approved a resolution to seek other Scottish Councils' support for their petition to Parliament for powers to rate land value. The Corporation prepared a bill to give effect to their petition. Conferences were called and the land values movement was built up in towns and cities throughout Britain. In the municipal elections in Glasgow out of a total of seventy-five councillors returned, forty-nine were in favour of the taxation of land values.

However, the idea was first raised in a parliamentary document when the Royal Commission on the Housing of the Working Classes advised in 1885 that a tax should be placed on unused land in the neighbourhood of towns.

George inspired a radical section of the younger Liberals, headed by Chamberlain and Morley, to link taxation with social policy. But that element of policy was eclipsed, first by the Home Rule movement for Ireland, and then by the return to power of the Conservatives from 1889 to 1906. As well as having little interest in social reform, their attention was absorbed by defending the Empire against the Boers in South Africa.

Between 1894–1900 there were 2835 public meetings held in Britain. Leaflets were distributed among working men's clubs, newspapers and to the signatories of petitions requesting the introduction of this reform. Red vans toured rural districts in Southern England in a campaign from 1891 to 1898. Yellow vans advocating their impractical policy of land nationalisation followed them. The opposition which the red vans met from landowners was proof that they were arousing agricultural workers. The Prime Minister, Lord Salisbury, warned electors in Exeter against people 'speaking from a van' who promised 'no end of profits to the voters if they would vote radical'.[1]

---

[1] E. Lawrence, *Henry George in the British Isles* p. 115.

Churchill, Member of Parliament

Sir Henry Campbell-Bannerman

A Dubious Invitation

Political unity - Balfour [Pragmatist], Hicks-Beach [Free Trader],
Chamberlain [Protectionist]

Morley, a leading Liberal, said at Forfar in October 1897, unearned increment from land was 'intolerable' and would be 'vigorously, powerfully, persistently, and successfully attacked . . . Now that is the kind of question which will no doubt try the House of Lords very hard, and when that question arises we shall see whether they will evade these [proposals for sweeping them away] by wisely bowing to the will of the people.'[1]

Land value taxation was promoted in London and Glasgow. In 1895 these cities held their first national conference for the taxation of land values. A bill prepared by the Glasgow Corporation was introduced in the House of Commons in 1899 but it failed to win a second reading. A Bill to impose land value rating in England was introduced into the House of Commons by Charles Trevelyan in 1902. It was defeated on Second Reading by a majority of 71. In 1904 he won a majority of 67 for a Bill of the same import. A Bill for Scotland was accorded a majority of 20 in 1905. There was considerable support among local government. Delegates were sent to the Commons from Glasgow, Liverpool, Manchester and Aberdeen. In England 518 authorities supported the rating of land values. A Select Committee was appointed under Alexander Ure K.C., then the Solicitor-General of Scotland, to look into a Scottish Bill introduced in 1906 by Mr Sutherland. They approved of the introduction of land value taxation and proposed that a separate valuation Bill be prepared for Scotland.

In December 1905 a petition for the introduction of land value rating, supported by 400 MPs, was presented to Campbell-Bannerman. He promised a Valuation Bill. He was fully behind the measure and had been an active supporter of it for several years. He had said at Keighley on 9 December 1902, 'Nothing short of taxation of land values will suffice to get at the root of this great matter [the distribution of wealth], so vitally essential to the health and prosperity of this country.' At Bedford on 15 October 1903, he said, 'We say that the land or rather the value that the community, by its aggregation, by its industry, by its public improvements, has given the land must be made to have its fair share of burdens now thrown upon our industry.' In Glasgow on 27 January 1904 he said, 'The rating of site values is not a mere question of the apportionment and incidence of the rates. It goes to the root of the most pressing and most neglected social questions.'[2] 'London presents present a group of problems of housing and overcrowding, problems of unemployment. The government would strengthen the hand of municipalities by reforming the land system & the rating system, in which, I include the imposition of a rate on ground values.'[3]

Churchill had shown shortly after his entry to Parliament that he had become a master of the principles of free trade. He had a contempt for the lack of fixity in argument and principle, which goes by the name of pragmatism: it is nothing but a suave name for the uncommitted mind which retains little gravitas, but

[1] *Times*, 7 October 1897.
[2] *Land Values*, June 1915 p .57.
[3] J. A. Spender, *The Life of Sir Henry Campbell-Bannerman* vol ii p. 209.

which reflects, like a glass mirror, every passing image. That mind is preoccupied with details and fashions, but it lacks dimension. Everything appears plausible. Churchill appears to have first become interested in the case for the Rating of Land Values after it was raised by Charles Trevelyan, a Liberal member who had introduced a bill concerning land value in the Commons in 1902 . His letter to Churchill was dated 31 December 1903. He was trying to make common ground with young Tories. He asked Churchill: 'Can you join us at all to relieve local taxation by a land value taxation? It is barely a party question, and all municipalities irrespective of party are with us on this principle'.[1] Churchill wrote to him on 17 October to list six key Liberal policies and land value taxation appeared second in his list. Clearly the question had assumed some definitive importance in his mind. On 12 November 1904 Trevelyan, wrote to him, referring to the paucity of material on the subject. Trevelyan stressed the benefits of the taxation of land value; the release of unused land, the subsequent fall in its value, the relief of industry from local taxation. Churchill replied on 17 November: 'Dear Charlie, Very many thanks for your kindness in forwarding me such a valuable and convenient budget on Land Values. I really must get to work to study it. I think you will have to give me some lessons.'[2]

Churchill loved large political ideas and taxation which involved more than any other question; definitely more than free trade. His letter to Trevelyan concluded, 'What a frightful muddle politics are in. The slatternly demoralisation of a democratic party untouched by a great personality or inspired by a lofty idea depresses me.'[3] A month later he thanked him for the walk and talk which they had enjoyed together. Churchill wrote to Trevelyan on 4 April 1906, while he was Under-Secretary for the Colonies, to say he had put Trevelyan's enquiry about taxation in the Colonies to his officials.

The principles of free trade seemed to Churchill exactly the same in 1904 as they had been in 1846. He showed a complete mastery of the concept of free trade and it may be presumed that he had acquired a similar mastery of the case for taxation. Later Churchill read George's work *Progress and Poverty*, after having borrowed a copy from the United Committee for the Taxation of Land Values. Andrew Maclaren, later active as a member of parliament in the cause of the land values movement, often used that copy, which had been marked in pencil by Churchill. It is clear from his formidable powers of comprehension and concentration that he was prepared to tackle a case of this scale.

While he was Colonial Secretary, 'Churchill', wrote Josiah Wedgewood, a Liberal member, '. . . stopped me behind the Speaker's Chair one day with: "Jos, I have been reading Henry George, and I must say I can see no answer to him." '[4]

---

[1] R. Churchill, *Winston Churchill* vol ii, Companion Pt. 2 p. 279.
[2] Trevelyan Papers, LPT 21.
[3] Trevelyan Papers.
[4] J. Wedgewood, *Memoirs of a Fighting Life* pp. 64–6.

The choice for a people is simple. Either they follow the natural order of society in which freedom, justice and prosperity are to be enjoyed by individual and community or they follow the order created by man and reap from his endless regulations and pious intentions the fruits of injustice, war and poverty. There is no doubt on which side Churchill stood on this question during the first decade of this century.

In 1906 Churchill embraced the two most powerful principles of political economy: free trade and just taxation. He stood poised for action. He had gained government office and yet preserved his independence of thought. His ability marched in step with his integrity. He was positioned to perform grand service to Britain and to mankind. For by ridding Britain of poverty and enabling her people to enjoy the fruits of liberty, this island could be a greater force in the world by virtue of her example than ever it had been by imperial possession.

In October 1908 Churchill consulted Edgar Harper, the Statistical Officer at the London County Council, on the question of taxation.

> Will you tell me how you meet this argument? All taxation falls on the person, not upon property. The burden of taxation is measured by the amount of sacrifice to any individual. The source of wealth is irrelevant, since wealth producing properties are freely and frequently interchangeable. There is no reason why a thousand a year from mining royalties should be taxed more heavily than a thousand a year from Consuls, except in so far as it can be shown that the property thus specially taxed is especially benefited by the consequent expenditure. The latter is the case in regard to land values, which would only be required to contribute proportionately to the process of its own enrichment.[1]

It was a rather obscure question, as Mr Harper showed in his reply. As there is a paucity of writing on the nature of property and taxation in British history, the reply merits quotation in full.

> 'Dear Mr Churchill,
>
> In answer to your letter, the argument quoted is inconclusive, because it has regard only to the first canon of taxation and does not reckon that canon by itself cannot be a guide to a satisfactory system of taxation. Absolute equality of burden or sacrifice is a chimera. No-one has been able to define it. Even if it were possible to achieve at a given moment, it is obvious that the transactions of the ensuing hour would destroy it.
>
> The argument appears to suggest that all kinds of wealth are equally fit subjects for taxation. But it is particularly impossible – even if it were

---

[1] Chartwell Papers 2/35, 31.

desirable – to tax all kinds of wealth. The question necessarily arises: On what principle a selection to be made? What standard should be set up to fix the citizen's contribution? In other words, what forms of wealth should be taxed?

It is true that, at the moment of paying, the amount of tax comes out of the taxpayer's bank balance. But it is useless to enquire whence that balance arises. In that sense 'the source of wealth is irrelevant'. But this does not dispose of the question – which is relevant and pertinent – what standard of contribution should be fixed, i.e. what kind of property should be taxed.

Here a number of considerations come in the vague ideas of equality, or sacrifice, and in particular the fourth canon that a good system of taxation should 'take and keep out of the pockets of the people as little as possible above what it brings in into the public treasury' – in other words it should not hinder the production and exchange of wealth.

The effect of taxation upon national poverty can hardly be overestimated, and its power in this respect is well expressed in the following quotation: 'Taxation may attack monopoly or it may diffuse wealth or it may concentrate it; it may promote liberty and equality of rights or it may tend to the establishment of tyranny; it may be used to bring about reforms or it may be so laid as to exaggerate existing grievances and foster hatred and dissension among classes; taxation may be so controlled by the skillful hand as to give free scope to every opportunity for the creation of wealth or for advancement of all true interests of states and cities, or it may be so sapped by ignorance as to place a dead weight on a community in the race or industrial supremacy.'[1]

The question how a tax affects national prosperity – hinders or encourages the production, exchange and consumption of wealth – depends mainly on the basis of the tax, the standard of contribution , the kind of property selected for taxation. This is the important point which must be borne in mind in addition to the ideals of equality of equality. A protective tariff might conceivably satisfy the test of approximating to equality of sacrifice, but the very practical objections are its unpardonable sins against the fourth canon.

Similarly, the really practical reason for taxing land values is that such a system would free and stimulate, instead of hampering, production and exchange. It will operate to prevent the holding of land out of use and will destroy the incentive to speculate in land. When all the land now unused is brought into the market the effect on labour will be most

---

[1] Prof. Ely.Taxation in America p. 55.

beneficial. Opportunities for employment – for using land – will be multiplied and the demand for labour will be increased. Moreover, the revenue produced by the tax will enable the State to relieve the necessaries of life from taxes which will bear upon them. House, and buildings of all kinds, machinery, sugar and the few items of imported food still paying duty will be freed from the burden and will consequently become cheaper. The purchasing power of wage will thus be further increased; and the working classes will have a wide margin of income to expend on comfort and recreation.

The tax would also, by eliminating speculation, tend to enable wealth to reach and remain in the hands that fairly earn it; securing not only free production but such a distribution of wealth as would accord with natural equity and national prosperity – exactly the reverse of the plunder and demoralisation which prevail under tariffs and powerful monopolies.

It would thus satisfy the fourth canon as no other system would – neither taking from the people nor causing to be taken from them more than the actual yield of the tax and the cost of its collection.

It would be simple, certain and direct in its incidence – convenient and easy to collect.

Lastly it would be the best approach of equality. It would reach all members of the community. All must make use of land and, in doing so, assist in its creating land value. The taxation of land value also assist in procuring most secure conditions for everyone, and this contribution from everyone, and this proportionate to the value of the natural advantage he enjoys. Between individuals this would be equity and justice that public wealth should be met out of the values created by the presence, industry and expenditure of the whole population.

The selection of particular items of property such as Consols, ground rents or mining royalties for special taxation is the very antithesis of the principle underlying the taxation of land value. They [mining royalties] differ from the economic 'rent of land' only by reason of the fact they were paid in respect of the actual extraction of a part of the land itself, and not in respect of its use in situ. For this reason the payment is proportional to the quantity extracted rather than the period of use. But it is just as much a payment for land value as the ground rent charged for a building site or any other rent of land. And I would not suggest that incomes from Consols should be taxed beyond other incomes other than that mining royalties or ground rents should be taxed beyond other forms of land value.

It is, however, essential to equity that all forms of land value – except that used by the community in common – should be taxed alike.

Whether the tax on any particular form of land value – such as ground rents or mining royalties should be payable by the receiver or payer depends altogether on the contract between them on that point. If there is no such contract the receiver should pay, because he enjoys the full value. If there is a contract, the party who binds himself to pay the taxes or rates must adhere to his bargain. Nor is this inequitable, for, in return for the undertaking to pay all rates and taxes to be charged upon the property, the lease a quid pro quo in the adjustment of the amount paid as ground rent or royalty.

With great respect, I remain your faithful and obedient servant.

Edgar Harper[1]

Harper became the chief valuer at the Inland Revenue in 1911.

---

[1] Chartwell Papers 2/35, 31.

5

Minister
1906–8

Campbell-Bannerman called a General Election immediately after taking over the government from Balfour. Balfour was thought too clever to have surrendered a position of advantage. It was widely believed by Conservatives that the Liberals would walk in and out of power as swiftly as they might enter only to leave immediately through a revolving door. At the time it was an understandable move. For Lord Rosebery, the former Liberal leader, had just spoken of a Liberal split over Ireland.

Campbell-Bannerman told his audience at the Albert Hall, London, on 21 December 1905 that:

> The government has executed what we call a moonlight flitting. It has run away, not in the broad light of session, not even in the twilight of October, but in the midnight of December.
>
> We are told – told emphatically and abundantly – that the manner of their going would be a masterpiece of tactical skill.
>
> Tactics! Tactics! Ladies and gentlemen, the country is tired of their tactics. It would have been better for them if they had less of tactics and more of reality.
>
> They have lived for some years on nothing but tactics. And now they have died of tactics. [In the same speech he added] We wish to make the land less of a pleasure-ground for the rich and more of a treasure-house for the nation.[1]

Balfour had misjudged the people's approval of free trade. Posters in the campaign contrasted free trade and protection as 'Big and little loaf'. Distrustful of the Tories 'food taxes, they hardly cared to hear his assertion that 'whether in power or whether in opposition the great Unionist Party will always control the destinies of this great Empire'. He was referring to the majority which his party

---

[1] J. Spender, *The Life of Sir Henry Campbell-Bannerman* vol ii p. 206 and p. 209.

maintained in the House of Lords, whom Lloyd George termed 'petrified Toryism'. Before the General Election there were in the House of Commons 355 Tory members, 124 Liberal Unionists and only 88 Liberals.

Churchill had moved from Oldham as the Liberal candidate to Manchester North-West [one of the six constituencies in the city], where he had become known during the promotion of the Aliens Bill in 1904. Manchester was the natural home for a free trader. Cobden and Bright had made it so in the days of the Anti-Corn Law League As he strode through the streets outside the Midland Hotel shortly after their arrival, he remarked to Marsh, 'Fancy living in one those streets – never seeing anything beautiful – never eating anything savory – never saying anything clever.'[1] As a Liberal candidate he opposed William Joynson-Hicks, a protectionist Tory who had issued a pamphlet listing Churchill's earlier sayings as a Tory. Churchill appeared at one meeting holding this derogatory pamphlet. He 'flung it from him with a dramatic gesture expressing contempt for the cause he had once espoused.' Later Churchill described his adversary by writing that 'the worst that can be said of him is he runs the risk of being most humorous when he wishes to be most serious.'[2] At one meeting the audience feared that a floor over an empty public bath would collapse. Churchill turned panic to laugher as he cried 'Let justice be done, even though the floor falls in'. He then proceeded with his speech and the floor held.

Churchill was never a snob and he revelled in poking fun at the social conventions of the Establishment. He distrusted the public schools and the conformity of thought and values which they instilled. He stood apart from this Englishness, probably on account of having had an American mother. Once a friend remarked that a young man was likely to take a First Class at Oxford and was about to be given his Rugby 'Blue'. 'What does that matter, asked Winston with withering scorn, 'whether he gets his Rugby Blue or his Rugby Green, or his Rugby dung-colour?'[3] For someone reared in such environs as Blenheim Palace, Manchester indeed seemed a different world.

'As this contest', Churchill declared during his election campaign, 'has the one dominant and decisive issue – Free Trade or Tariff Reform – it has become increasingly plain . . . In twenty years time nothing will be remembered about this election except that it settled whether the fiscal policy of Mr Cobden & Sir Robert Peel was or was not to be repudiated.'[4] The Liberals fought under the slogan, *Support the Liberal Party and the Taxation of Land Values.*

In his Address to the voters of Manchester North-West, Churchill set out his programme : free trade, religious equality, the public control of education, reduction of expense on armaments, the taxation of land values, trade union law

[1] R. Churchill, *Winston S. Churchill* vol ii p. 113.
[2] Ibid p. 114.
[3] Earl of Birkenhead, *Churchill 1874–1922* p. 60.
[4] *Times* 1 January 1907.

reform and liquor licensing reform. He also delivered his final attack on the former Conservative government.

> Under its hand the procedure of the House of Commons has been mutilated, and has been notably and notoriously diminished. Jealous of nothing, save the leisure of its members it has bartered Parliamentary rights for longer holidays and easier hours of session, and has shirked urgent business at the prompting of personal indolence. Viewy, intolerant, dilettante, lax, the tool of Whips and wire-pullers, the lackey of private interests. The Parliament of 1900 had grudged the freedom of speech, conspired against the freedom of trade, parodied the freedom and dignity of labour ... It is upon the strength of such performances and testimonials that Mr Balfour and Mr Chamberlain rudely claim renewal of their lease. Do not be taken in again.[1]

In that address Churchill met the weak argument that declaration of free trade opened the nation to the vicious international blockade against British, or indeed, against trade itself. 'I do not accept a policy of retaliation [against other nations]; for I believe with Sir Robert Peel in fighting hostile imports by free imports'.[2]

To suppose that the trading power of a trading nation depends on its exports is to misconceive the nature of trade. It as ridiculous as pretending that the life of an individual depends only of exhaling breath. It is the exact reverse in both instances. The need of imports is indeed the great strength of British trade. All that parliament need concern itself with is whether there is freedom of imports. It does not matters that the entire globe is shut against British exports. For in that case there can be no imports because the British people cannot export and thus pay for them.

The campaign was marred by militant suffragettes. Churchill was often heckled and faced with the question of where he stood on the issue. He said he had voted in favour of one Bill in the Commons, but, having seen the destructive force of the suffragettes he was not induced to accede to their demands. When one heckler had been summoned to the platform to put her question, answered and then ejected Churchill told his cheering audience, 'that he was not going to be hen-pecked'. As a Cabinet minister he was a prime target for the suffragettes who harried him until the First War at every election.

The General Election was held in January 1906. The whole process of voting and counting was spread over three weeks. The former Conservative regime was struggling for a return to power and the Liberals were hoping for a decisive victory. The election of 1906 recorded the largest landslide in history. 'Here', he

---

[1] Ibid.
[2] Ibid p. 125.

wrote, 'the whole apparatus of Protection, so laboriously rebuilt has been overthrown; paraphrasing Mr Pitt's famous sentence after Trafalgar, I may say "Manchester has saved itself by her own exertions and, will, I trust, save England by her example." ' When his result was declared on 13 January 1906 he was much in demand where polling had not yet been completed. It was a huge adventure for Churchill. His personality outweighed free trade as the main topic in Manchester. Even his taste in hats caught the eye.

The election was, according to Churchill, 'the most vehement expression of public opinion'. Meetings were well attended and speeches were often reported in full. In an electorate of four and a half million, the Liberals achieved a majority of over 300,000 votes. Liberals held 377 seats and the Unionists only 157. The Irish Nationalists held 83 seats and the Labour Party 53, whose emergence as a political force was evidence that the British electorate were dissatisfied with the order of the previous century. So the Liberals commanded an overall majority of 84 and when the two minority parties voted with them, as they often did, the majority over the Unionists swelled to a massive 356. F. E. Smith, a Conservative Member, likened the avalanche of Liberal members 'floating into Parliament like corks on top of a dirty wave'. Indeed 300 were new to Parliament. Among the defeated was Balfour at Manchester North-East, where he lost by 2000 votes. He was returned to Parliament shortly afterwards for another seat, which was vacated for him.

Campbell-Bannerman, the Liberal Prime Minister, chose a government which was described as one 'of all talents': Asquith, Edward Grey, Morley, Richard Haldane, Crewe, John Bryce, Augustine Birrell and Lloyd George. The Cabinet included a Socialist John Burns, the first of them to attain Cabinet rank, as President of the Local Government Board. He had been a leader at the disorderly meeting, which broke up in violence, in Trafalgar Square in 1885. On his appointment Burns said, 'Sir 'Enery, this is the most popular thing you 'ave done.'[1] Burns enjoyed a lively understanding with the king, who liked colourful and straight-forward characters. When showing guests round his smoking room, the king drew their attention to the one chair made special by being sat upon by Burns. Churchill had been appointed Under-Secretary for the Colonies in December 1905, before Election and held the position after it.

The Prime Minister had acquired his cumbersome name by adding the surname of his uncle, as required under his will. He disliked it and preferred to style himself C-B. 'With his mutton chops', wrote Colin Cross,' and his detached manner, he looked more like an official than a politician. Yet by temperament and conviction Campbell-Bannerman was probably the truest radical ever to become Prime Minister of Great Britain.'[2] He commanded respect and friendship effortlessly.

---

[1] D. Barden, *Churchill in Parliament* p. 49.
[2] C. Cross *The Liberals in Power* p. 12.

'Simplicity, candour, honesty and good humour', wrote a contemporary, 'just a little touch of commonplaceness which makes the whole world in the street kin; he was able to inspire a personal devotion and affection which might have been impossible to men of more commanding and dominating powers.'[1]

There was an agreement among Asquith, Grey and Haldane and the king that the Prime Minister should go to the House of Lords and leave Asquith in charge of the Commons. Yet, after discussing the plan with his wife, Campbell-Bannerman did not agree. He had not yet received an opinion from Dr Ott, his personal physician, in Marienbad, who advised that he should go to the Lords, in order to safeguard his health. He, therefore, resolved to remain in the Commons. Asquith immediately backed out of the agreement once he heard of the Prime Minister's decision and the idea was dropped. Soon he was exerting real leadership outside Parliament, as well as in Cabinet and Party. He proved himself to be the leader the like of which no one had suspected. '. . . in many trying passages of public life', wrote Morley, 'he had shown unshaken courage, invincible independence even of public opinion itself, steadfast adherence to his own political principles in spite of busy and untoward dissents inside his party.'[2]

Unfortunately his effectiveness was, unhappily, reduced by illness. His wife, Charlotte suddenly died in August 1906. He had been devoted to her during their forty-six years of marriage. He had nursed her even if state duties had to be cancelled or postponed. She refused to be served in bed by her nurses; her food and every want had to be provided by her husband. He was shaken by her death. On the anniversary of her death Arthur Ponsonby, a private secretary, found him with his head held in his hands sobbing with uncontrolled grief.

He had no liking for Balfour, now Leader of the Opposition. After Balfour had entertained the House with his characteristic and pointless dexterity he replied in the spirit of the new mood wrought by the election.

> The Right Honourable Gentleman is like the Bourbons in the oft-quoted phrase – he has learnt nothing. He comes to this new House of Commons with the same airy grace, the same subtle dialectics, the same light and frivolous way of treating a great question, but he little knows the temper of the new House of Commons if he thinks these methods will prevail here . . . His questions to me are utterly futile, nonsensical and misleading. They are invented by the Right Honourable Gentleman for the purpose of occupying time in this debate. I say enough of this foolery . . . move your amendments and let us get to business.[3]

Philip Snowden, a Labour Member, was impressed with the performance of the

---

[1] T. P. O'Connor, *Campbell-Bannerman* p. 90.
[2] John Morley, *Reflections* vol. 2 p. 141.
[3] A. Maurois, *King Edward and His Times* p. 284.

Prime Minister. 'This telling speech lasted only four minutes, but it was one of the most effective I ever heard in the House of Commons. It aroused the House to a frenzy of enthusiasm.'[1] His opinion was widely shared.

Campbell-Bannerman had the attributes of a statesman. He commanded the House of Commons by his presence alone. The secret of his power, according to his friend T. P. O'Connor lay not in arrogance, domination, oratory or play-acting. 'But at bottom the man is sincere, frank, and thorough. And it is this that accounts for his power over his followers'.[2] Balfour, however, thought the Prime Minister unpolished.

Churchill shone in Parliament with a rare brilliance. He recognised a similar quality in F. E. Smith, a distinguished lawyer, as a kindred spirit. Whereas it seemed that Churchill had been endowed, FE had earned his unusual abilities. He had entered the Commons as a Unionist in 1906, having established himself at the Bar. 'It was only after the Parliament had run some months of its course', Churchill recalled, 'that we were introduced to one another . . . From that hour our friendship was perfect. It was one of my most precious possessions. It was never disturbed by the fiercest party fighting.'[3] Smith dismissed the criticisms of Churchill's truculence and aggression in a few words of appreciation. He wrote '. . . no man living is more tolerant more easy, more companionable, in social intercourse. And his charm and friendship are as well known as his genius.'

Smith had gambled his political career on his maiden speech in 1906. On the way to the Commons he told his wife his speech might fall flat and, since he was not prepared to become a party time-server, he might have to abandon politics. His humour, however, caught the ear of the House and he was immediately established. Churchill admired that spirit and courage. He also was impressed with the ease with which FE could deliver a speech of an hour without hesitation or note. FE commanded his special admiration for his mental dexterity. 'For all purposes of discussion, argument, exposition, appeal or altercation', Churchill remembered, 'FE had a complete armoury. The bludgeon for the platform; the rapier for all personal disputes; the entangling net and unexpected trident for the Courts of Law; and a jug of clear spring water for an anxious, perplexed conclave.'[4] Years later Morley predicted that Lord Birkenhead, as FE was to become, would lead the government in the Lords, while Churchill would lead in the Commons.

Spender, editor of the *Westminster Gazette*, years later wrote of his impression of Churchill in 1906.

> Churchill is endowed by nature with the most rhetorical mind that I have known in any public man . . . To discuss a question with Churchill was

---

[1] Viscount Snowden, *An Autobiography vol* i p. 139.
[2] J. Wilson, *A Life of Sir Henry Campbell-Bannerman* p. 513.
[3] WSC, *Contemporary Contemporaries* p. 109.
[4] Ibid p. 110.

to see him dramatise it in successive scenes with effective lights and colours, and then at the end choose the scene which was best dramatised and most effectively lit. It was fascinating to watch him at work painting the scenery and building up the wings, but at times one had an uneasy feeling that truth and practicability and even common sense were left behind in this breathless chase after the picturesque. Nothing seemed to appeal to him unless it could be presented in this form, and he appeared to be capable of leaping from one side of an argument to its opposite without the slightest sense of incongruity, if the opposite lent itself to a more effective plastic treatment . . . Churchill had . . . first-class wits and a remarkable power of inspiring fear in those whom it is important to conciliate.[1]

The immediate question to be settled in Churchill's department of Colonial Affairs was peace in South Africa after the Boers had accepted defeat in 1902. The restoration of peace was the great achievement of the Prime Minister, C-B. The war had distressed him in 1900 he had likened Kitchener's policy to a pheasant shoot and called the tactics employed 'methods of barbarism'. Louis Botha, who became Prime Minister of South Africa , believed that those 'three words made peace and union in South Africa' C-B insisted on a policy of understanding and generosity when he came to power and Churchill agreed with both sentiments. General Smuts recalled C-B many years later: '. . . a wise man with profound feeling and profound political instinct who achieved one of the wisest political settlements in the history of this nation.'[2]

As part of the solution of the troubles in South Africa it fell to Churchill to implement the Cabinet's decision on the constitution for the Orange River and the Transvaal colonies. Churchill had assumed the measure would be handled by the Prime Minister himself. The previous government had administered both regions directly from London as Crown colonies. Churchill found himself facing Chamberlain, who had been the Conservative Colonial Secretary.

No sooner had the [Boer] War' come to an end [said Churchill] than the Right Honourable Gentleman got tired of the South African situation, pushed it away from him as a toy which had ceased to amuse, and embarked at once upon another adventure which was as rash and as uncalculated as the first, and the only difference between the two was that, whereas the first enterprise of the Right Honourable Gentleman has had the effect of nearly ruining South Africa, the second enterprise has had the effect of politically ruining himself.[3]

[1] J. A. Spender *Life, Journalism and Politics*, 163–4.
[2] J. Morley *Reflections*, vol. 2 p. 145.
[3] *Hansard*, 21 March 1906.

Churchill put the immediate choice for the Government succinctly in a memorandum: 'The vital and fundamental issue is this: who is to govern the Transvaal Colony; are we to govern through selected officers, or are the inhabitants of the Transvaal to govern it through elected representatives?' He urged the grant of responsible self-government, whereby the government would become responsible to its electors. Votes were given to male whites. 'No law will be assented to which sanctions any condition of service or residence of a servile character,' Churchill assured in statesmanlike fashion.

It was a busy first session for Churchill in Parliament, owing partly to the fact from May C-B had been unable to introduce legislation on South Africa into the Commons because nursing his wife became a priority. He wrote to the king to describe himself as busier over the South African situation in the House of Commons than any Member of the Government, save Birrell, who was handling the Education Bill.

The previous government had allowed the recruitment of Chinese labour to work in South African gold mines under severe contracts of slavery. These contracts, which allowed a number of distasteful practices including flogging, became extremely unpopular in Britain. About 50,000 coolies had been recruited by 1906. Churchill decided to allow this contract to expire after its life, rather than declare it illegal. However distasteful the Chinese Contract might appear, Churchill was not prepared to set contractual relations aside. Churchill used his power with words to get out of a tight corner. 'It [the Contract] cannot, in the opinion of Her Majesty's Government be classified as slavery in the extreme acceptance of the word without some risk of terminological inexactitude.' No new contracts were written and he introduced more humane conditions meantime.

Balfour denounced the granting of self-government to the Transvaal as 'the most reckless experiment ever tried in the development of a great colonial policy'.[1] It would certainly have been defeated in the House of Lords, had it been included in a Bill. But it was effected under Letters Patent, or by a grant from the sovereign, and their Lordships were not, therefore, allowed to vent their dislike of Liberalism.

In addition to South Africa, the Colonial Office administered sixty colonies throughout the Empire. The fifth Colonial Conference had to be arranged for a meeting in London and conducted in April 1907. Seven premiers attended. The Conference decided that self-governing colonies were henceforth to be known as 'dominions'. Concluding his address to the conference Churchill touched on the tariff reform argument which had taken hold of the principal members.

It has been a source of regret to all on this subject we cannot come to an agreement. A fundamental difference of opinion on economics, no

---

[1] Hansard 30 July 1907 vol 162 col 804.

doubt, makes agreement impossible; but although we regret that, I do not doubt that in the future, when Imperial unification has been carried to a stage which it is now not reached, and will not, perhaps, in our time attain, people in that more fortunate age will look back to the Conference of 1907 as a date in the history of the British Empire when one grand wrong turn was successfully avoided.

Churchill got on well with his departmental minister, Lord Elgin, who had served as Viceroy in India, where he has been described as 'weak and colourless'.[1] He was nearing the end of his political career. There were minor disagreements between the two men but no serious argument. Indeed it is a tribute to so young a public servant as Churchill that he was able to conduct himself in the House of Commons without slip, apart from his clumsy first ministerial speech.

In July 1906 Chamberlain had a stroke and the weakness of his voice and loss of motive power effectively ended his career. Tariff reform was left lingering in the air. Tariff reform or protectionism had a timeless allure for Unionists and later for Socialists and later even for Liberals. In October 1906 Churchill declined the invitation of the Young British Liberals to speak in the Town Hall of Birmingham while his friend lay stricken.

Churchill was preoccupied with his political career, yet he was free of conceit. There was an engaging, almost childlike quality, in his enthusiasms, which he revealed in a conversation in 1906 with Violet Asquith. 'He turned on me a lowering gaze and asked me abruptly how old I was. I replied I was nineteen. "And I", he said almost despairingly, "am thirty-two already. Younger than anyone else who counts, though." ' After a long diatribe on human mortality and the transitory appearances of the world, he concluded, "We are all worms, but I do believe I am a glow worm." '[2] That he was ambitious and loved being in the limelight was patently evident. But his charm, his enthusiasm, his friendship and his humour were always generous and free of conceit and snobbery. He eschewed the social life of dinners and dances which captivated his brother, Jack, with whom he lived in Mayfair.

On 25 January 1907 the Prime Minister visited his native city of Glasgow to receive the Freedom of the City. Indeed was the inspiration of his radicalism and the city had real warmth for their son. 'What is the use', he asked, 'of all our wealth and learning and the finest flower of our civilisation and our constitution, what are those and our political theories but dust and ashes, if the men and women on whose labour the whole social fabric is maintained are doomed to live and die in darkness and misery in the recesses of our great cities?'[3]

---

[1] P. Moon, *The British Conquest and Dominion of India* p. 902.
[2] V. Bonham Carter *Churchill as I Knew Him* p,16–17.
[3] *Glasgow Herald* 26 January 1907.

The King's Speech to Parliament in early 1907 highlighted the immediate issue confronting the Liberal Government, 'Serious questions affecting the working of our parliamentary system have arisen from the unfortunate division of the two Houses. My ministers have this important subject under consideration with a view to the solution of the difficulty.'[1] Yet no practical steps were announced.

The Lords had been obstructive to the government's legislative programme throughout 1906. The Education Bill, proposing to bringing elementary schools maintained from public funds under public control; the Plural Voting Bill, seeking to abolish multiple votes; and the Aliens Bill, aiming to impose controls on foreign labour during times of distress, were either wrecked or rejected. Also the Education (Provision of Meals) Act, the Agricultural Holdings and the Town Tenants (Ireland) Act were each mutilated.

In February 1907 Churchill spoke at the Manchester Free Trade Hall on the veto which the House of Lords claimed. He drew attention to

> the plain absurdities in the composition of our hereditary chamber where a man acquires legislative functions simply through his virtue of being born, where the great majority of the members never come near the place from year's end to year's end, where if they go mad or are convicted of a crime or become mentally incompetent to manage their estates or acquire an unwholesome acquaintance with intoxicating beverages, nevertheless they are still entitled to sit.[2]

In March a Bill was re-introduced for land value taxation in Scotland, an earlier attempt having failed in the previous Parliament. This time the Government referred it to a Select Committee under Alexander Ure K.C., the Solicitor-General of Scotland. The Committee approved of the introduction of land value taxation and proposed that a separate valuation Bill be prepared for Scotland. Such a Bill would empower local authorities to raise finance from the value of land, in the place of rates.

On 20 April 1907 the 280 Liberal Members of Parliament favouring land value taxation called mass demonstrations in London. Churchill spoke to an audience estimated at 4000 at the Drury Lane Theatre. There were 150 Members on the platform. It was an occasion made for Churchill's colourful and powerful rhetoric. He did not

> suppose there was ever a moment in the whole of our lives when the prospects of land reform looked brighter or rosier than they did to-day. [Cheers]. It was no light thing they were going to do. They had pulled up

---

[1] Hansard vol 167 col 3.
[2] *Times* 5 February 1907.

the curtain on a piece that was going to have a long run. He observed that a very distinguished man attributed the migration of the agricultural men to the towns on account of their love of amusements. [Laughter] The motive which inspired the agricultural labourer to exchange a cheerful life in the countryside with 14s a week and the workhouse at the end of it, the squalor of city slums was not rollicking hilarity. [Laughter]. If there was a steady stream of the best men from the villages into towns it was because, as the Prime Minister had said, they could not call their souls their own. [Loud cheers]. They wanted to be free men, to rise in the world by their own resources, and the country had no career for them. [A voice: 'Perfectly true' and cheers]

The movement for land reform aimed, not at the redistribution of existing wealth, but at the discovery of new springs of production ... There was no intention of plundering the landlord, and there was intention of allowing him to plunder us. [Cheers] They did not want to take from any class that which belonged to it; but they were resolved if they could ... to prevent any class from steadily absorbing under the shelter of the law the wealth in the creation of which they had borne no share – wealth which belonged not to them but to the community – wealth which they could only secure by vexatious obstruction of social and economic progress – far more injurious and wasteful than could be measured by their own inordinate gain ... Our rating system is a patchwork of perversity. [Laughter][1]

In Manchester the Prime Minister delighted in the attitude of his adversaries.

A kind of frenzy seizes the Unionist party whenever it is proposed to touch the land, and the Leader of the Opposition has already badly fallen victim to this frenzy, and we must see this form of seizure spreading ... I do not care whether it is in extending the facilities for the labourers to cultivate the land, or to acquiring land for cottages, or in increasing the security of tenure for the farmer, or in readjusting the incidence of local taxation in such a way to secure for the community the future increment its own improvements I am afraid, we shall be held up as a set of low-bred fellows, fit company for poachers.

Churchill was made a Privy Councillor in May 1907. In uniform and with his sword he was a splendid figure. But Herbert Samuel, a fellow minister, told how evidently he detested the uniform which showed in its gold embroidery on the collar and cuffs – the higher order of Councillor had a plain rather than a serrated

---

[1] *Times* 22 April 1907.

edge – his station as only a junior minister. It was, Churchill insisted, pointing to his sleeve, 'The badge of shame!'[1]

In Edinburgh in May Churchill predicted that more employment of the power of veto by the Lords over bills which had passed the Commons 'would forever destroy their veto'.

The government had reintroduced an Education Bill in 1907. It sought to place all state-aided elementary schools under the control of local government, that is out of the control of the churches and it sought to limit religious instruction in these schools to Bible reading. To a reasonably disinterested person such a measure might have seemed mild and sensible. Furthermore, elementary schooling was in need of reform: classes were too large, teachers were poorly trained and education seemed irrelevant to the promotion of intelligence or industry. The education of a young soul was an opportunity for a church in the same way a sick patient represented the prospect of fees to an ambulance-chasing doctor. They admired the Jesuits' claim that if they were given the child's mind they would produce the man that Ignatius Loyola, their founder, had dreamed of rearing. School had long been regarded the nursery of the church.

Yet the Education Bill, along with the Trades Disputes Bill and the Plural Voting Bill, had to pass Balfour's strategy for the control of Parliament, which involved the overwhelming majority of Conservative peers in the Lords coming to the rescue of Conservative minority in the Commons. It was anchored to the large majority which his party maintained in the Lords. There were 602 peers and only about 90 were reckoned to be loyal Liberals. His basic approach was described in a letter to Lord Lansdowne, the Leader of the House of Lords, who had been his fag master at Eton, 'I incline to advise that we should fight all points of difference to oppose a measure very stiffly in the Commons and employ the House of Lords as a theatre of compromise.'[2] Thus the Unionists could bring into use their majority in the Upper House to compensate for their weakness in the Lower House. Lansdowne saw the Unionists in both Houses as 'two wings of the army'. Like its author, this approach was intellectually elegant, but tended to lack substance and principle.

The strategy was applied to the Trades Disputes Bill, which freed the trade unions from their legal liability under common law while conducting a trade dispute. The House of Lords, sitting judicially, had recently overturned the Court of Appeal in the Taff Valley railway case. They had held that a trades union was liable in civil law for damages caused by their dispute. There was no strong principle in the Bill to suspend the common law; just a desire of both main parties to enlist the support of the trades unions. So the House of Lords, acting legislatively, permitted their amendments to this Bill to be ignored. F. E. Smith

[1] *Winston Spencer Churchill Servant of Crown and Commonwealth* p. 49.
[2] Lord Newton, *Lord Landowne, a Biography* p. 355.

voted against this measure on principle and he ridiculed the pretension that at common law the trade unions had enjoyed an immunity from tortuous liability.

Balfour's legislative strategy was scrapped after its initial trial and the Lords rejected the Plural Voting Bill outright, without more than two hours of debate on its Second Reading. As it sought to cancel the right of the wealthy to exercise more than one vote, it was a deeply emotive measure. A man of property was, surely, their Lordships felt, entitled to vote wherever he happened from time to time to reside.

This left the Education Bill. It sought to bring elementary schooling maintained at public expense under the public control of a rating authority; in other words away from its control by the church. There were the Non-conformist ratepayers on the one side and the devout Church on the other. It was understandably a contentious issue.

Balfour was an agnostic and, therefore, not motivated by profound sentiment. It was not a subject which interested the Prime Minister. He told his secretary: 'What the French call "terrain vague" – weeds, broken bottles, no fence . . . One must cover its vagueness by an excess of platitudinous zeal.'[1] Conspiring with the Leader of the Unionist peers, Lord Lansdowne, Balfour decided to follow the advice of Randall Davidson, the Archbishop of Canterbury. He advised that the Education Bill be so heavily amended that he could leap in, as a *deus ex machina*, with a compromise which would still leave the Church of England in control of elementary education. But he did not like seeing the largest electoral majority set at nought by what Churchill called 'this frivolous, lethargic, uninstructed and disreputable' body in the Lords.[2] In early December 1906 the Government rejected the Lords' amendments to the Education Bill and was minded to end this Balfourian foolery. The Prime Minister asked in the House of Commons 'Is the General Election to go for nothing? . . . the resources of the British Constitution are not wholly exhausted . . .'[3] His desire to hold an immediate General Election was opposed by his Cabinet. He was forced to face the unreformed House of Lords and the negative collusion of the fag master and his fag for another session.

Balfour found his Lordship useful but he had a modest opinion of him as a man. He told a friend that he was 'not very clever . . . better than competent'. His Lordship had been Foreign Secretary and Viceroy in India. 'Lord Lansdowne's Viceroyalty', observed Moon, '. . . fell within a tranquil period of comparative prosperity and complacency, and except for one minor sensational episode was uneventful'.[4] Lansdowne bequeathed five years of troubles in India for Lord Elgin, his successor in the sub-continent.

The Prime Minister appointed a Cabinet committee to consider how best to deal

---

[1] J. Wilson, *A Life of Sir Henry Campbell-Bannerman* p. 555.
[2] Article in *The Nation* 2 May 1907.
[3] Hansard 20 Dec 1907 vol 167 col 1739-40.
[4] P. Moon, *The British Conquest and Dominion of India* p. 892.

with the House of Lords' veto. They reported after four months with a complex scheme for joint conferences at which the government would enjoy a majority, provided only they had a majority of over 100 in the Commons. The Prime Minister rejected such a constitutional hotchpot and revived the idea of a suspensory veto, as first promulgated by John Bright at Birmingham in August 1884. The Lords would be able to veto a measure sent up by the Commons twice, but after a third veto the measure became law. It was simple and decisive.

Churchill also turned his powerful beam on the defeated Leader of the Unionists:, 'Mr Balfour is no longer Prime Minister of this country. He sits in Opposition, in a lonely, solitary place on the left behind the Speaker's chair. But he has power. He has power to write a note . . . and give it to a messenger and send it 200 yards down the corridor to the House of Lords. And by writing that note, he can mutilate or reject or pass into law any clause or any bill which the House of Commons may have spent several weeks discussing . . .'[1] Churchill ridiculed Wyndham's idea that the Lords were like an umpire.

> It looks to me like the attitude of the footpad who waits for a dark night to stab his enemy rather than the act of an impartial chamber of review . . . We have got to pass one or two radical budgets first. We have got to formulate our policy upon the land first. . . . The battle between the Lords and Commons has to be fought out in Parliament first – then it will be fought out afterwards in the country. A great constitutional issue has been raised.[2]

Henry Chaplin, a Conservative Member, likened the House of Lords to a watch dog of the Constitution. Such a preposterous claim drew the the attention of Lloyd George. It was, he said: 'Mr Balfour's poodle; it fetches and carries for him; it bites anyone he sets it onto.'[3] The King was incensed when Lloyd George asked a meeting at Oxford whether the country should be governed by the King or peers or the King and is people. He did not want the sovereign's name to be brought into 'these vicious tirades of his'.[4] However, this warning could not restrain the oratory of Lloyd George and was the first of many royal interventions.

Since suffering a sudden loss of memory towards the end of a speech in the Commons in 1904 Churchill always made a point of thoroughly rehearsing a speech and of writing it out. There were advantages and disadvantages of preparing a speech. Balfour contrasted both: 'The Rt. Hon. Gentleman's artillery is very powerful, but it is not very mobile. It fires away at positions we never held.'

---

[1] R. Churchill, *Winston S. Churchill* vol ii p. 319.
[2] Ibid. pp. 319–20.
[3] E. T. Raymond, *Lloyd George* p. 102.
[4] J. Wilson, *A Life of Sir Henry Campbell-Bannerman* p. 556.

Asquith, the Chancellor of the Exchequer, was a lawyer by habit and a scholar by natural inclination. He was not a likely character to provide the spark of a constitutional explosion. Indeed his second Budget in April 1907 was not the measure for which the Cabinet was in need in order to break out of the legislative stranglehold imposed them. In an intellectual way, it was revolutionary, even exciting perhaps. It was an innovative but cautious budget for, as he pointed out, 'behind and beyond this [financial arithmetic] lies the whole still unconquered territory of social reform . . . The Chancellor of the Exchequer, in other words, ought to budget not for one year but several years.'[1] Asquith agreed with the select committee in distinguishing between earned and unearned income. He laid the foundations of the Old Age Pensions. 'Whatever is done in this matter must be done by steps and stages and cannot be achieved at a single blow.' By April 1908 he would have £2.25 million plus additional sums from increased estate duties to apply to old-age pensions.

Bills of secondary importance escaped the veto of the fag master and his peers. Bills to create a Territorial Army, to create the Criminal Appeal Court and to enable widowers to marry their wife's sister were let through. But in May 1907 the government unloosed the Small Holdings Bill, which sought greater security for small tenant farmers, and the Land Values (Scotland) Bill, which sought to place local taxation on land value. The Prime Minister declared at Manchester on 9 May that he would not allow the Lords to turn a majority in the Commons into a minority, 'The present House of Commons was not elected to pass only such Bills as commend themselves to the House of Lords. None of his Majesty's Ministers appealed for support on the ground that the programme . . . was subject to whatever discount might be placed on it in another House. This is a Liberal Government and a Liberal House of Commons, elected by an overwhelming Liberal and Progressive majority to pass Liberal measures, and we should be unworthy of the confidence placed in us . . . if we allowed ourselves to forget who placed us where we are, and whence we derive the authority, the sanction, and the impetus for our proposals.'[2]

Speaking about the Government's land policy, Churchill said, 'Happy shall we be if to us it is given to disperse the cloud of gloom which has settled over our villages, to enable the peasantry to lift up their heads and call their souls their own, by giving them little footholds where they will no longer be tied men but free; happy shall we be before our day is over we see some brightness and colour and pleasant homes for the people in our cities, and vigorous well nourished children playing in the gardens of our cities instead of in dismal and sunless streets, which are too often the only playgrounds given to them.'[3]

The first bill was an irritating measure to their Lordships. Lord Lansdowne spoke

---

[1] *Times* 19 April 1907.
[2] *Liberal Magazine* June 1907 p. 322.
[3] Chartwell Papers 2/31, 2.

for his landlord fellows, 'What gives reality', he averred with conviction, 'to ownership of land and makes it a valuable and precious thing is to many people, above all, the right to select persons to be associated with the proprietor in the cultivation of the soil. That is to me the true relationship between landlord and tenant.'[1] The Prime Minister thought this notion 'picturesque' and 'pleasant'.[2] This was so important a deliberation that could not be delegated by the few who owned land. The second bill was more offensive and it was rejected. Speaking in Edinburgh in October 1907 the Prime Minister derided the rejection as a 'piece of arrogance and high-handedness which went to the extreme points of pretensions of he House of Lords ... [They] know about the affairs in Edinburgh, and the affairs of Manchester and Glasgow and how they should be managed ... Shall we learn something – possibly we may, and it may give us a little hope – from what I call the parable of Westminster Bridge? You may remember how the House of Lords decided that the tramways from the south must not be brought across the bridge almost under their windows. They thought it better that the people who cross the bridge in their thousands and tens of thousands should trudge on foot to and from their work. But the Lords were subsequently frightened by the outcry which their proceedings has raised ... now the majority of the House of Lords is daily outraged by the spectacle of crowded tramway cars. (Cheers and laughter)'[3]

The Prime Minister deplored this farce; the Lords were arrogating to themselves an authority which prevailed over the people's mandate. He passed the following resolution in the Commons on 24 June 1907: 'That, in order to give effect to the will of the people, as expressed by their elected representatives, it is necessary that the power of the other House to alter or reject bills passed by this House should be so restricted by law as to secure within the limits of a single Parliament the final decision of the House of Commons will prevail.'[4] The resolution was designed to fire a warning shot at the Upper House. No concrete proposals were tabled.

Balfour argued in a speech given in October 1907 that power was vested in the House of Lords, not to prevent the people of this country having the laws they wished, but to see that the laws were not the hasty and ill-considered offspring of a passionate election.

Advising a young Liberal who appears to have procured his goodwill under false pretences, Churchill revealed his manly approach to politics in his reply. 'The Liberal cause will gain enormously in strength and dignity by being utterly dissociated with anything like rowdyism or dodgery. Use the grand argument, appeal to history; appeal to economics; appeal to science.'[5]

---

[1] *The Liberal Magazine* Nov 1907 p. 624.
[2] Ibid.
[3] *Times, 7 Oct 1907.*
[4] Hansard vol 176 col 98.
[5] Chartwell Papers 2/34, 57.

In the summer of 1907 the Prime Minister did not go for a holiday to Marienbad, as he done for the past twenty years with his late wife. Since her death he had been lonely. Instead he went to his home in Scotland and was determined to resolve the issue of the Lords during his holiday. In the autumn he spoke publicly on the issue and undertook a heavy schedule of engagements. At a meeting at Bristol in November forward he dismissed the House of Lords as a protector of abuse and privilege and looked forward to the will and the capacity of the country: 'to move quietly steadily forward along the path of social reform towards a fairer and more enlightened common life, free from the disgrace of the existence of unnecessary and unmerited misery and poverty.'[1] The meeting had tired him and had been frequently interrupted by suffragettes. That night he sustained a more serious heart attack. His life hung in the balance for two hours. It could not be concealed from the public any longer. Two weeks later he went to recover in Biarritz until January 1908.

In the summer recess of 1907 Churchill embarked on an unofficial trip through Europe to East Africa and this adventure occupied him until early in January 1908. He described in letters to his mother his excitement of shooting large game. In Kenya, he wrote, 'On turning round the hill we saw, almost five hundred yards away, a rhinoceros grazing quietly. I cannot describe to you the impression produced on the mind by the sight of the grim black silhouette of this mighty beast – a survival of prehistoric times – roaming about the plain as he & his forerunners had done since the dawn of the world.'[2] He shot at another, hit it, but did not kill it, and the beast charged him.

He earned the considerable sum of £1150 by submitting a series of five articles to *Strand Magazine*. These articles were published in book form, entitled *My African Journey*.

Writing to his mother about the funeral of a dear servant, 'I thought as I walked after the coffin ... how easily it might have been ... me ... I suppose there is some work for me to do.'[3] Churchill had not followed the weary wisdom of aged-Harcourt, who had warned against expecting anything to happen in life.

---

[1] *Times*, 14 November 1907.
[2] R. Churchill, *Winston S. Churchill* vol ii Companion Pt. 2 p. 693.
[3] Ibid. p. 738.

6

Cabinet
1908–10

There had been no autumn session of Parliament. Churchill hurried back from South Africa to learn that the Prime Minister's health had deteriorated after a heart attack six weeks earlier. After his return from holiday Campbell-Bannerman tried to appear fit again. But in Cabinet he tired visibly. The legislative programme, which was announced in the King's Speech in February 1908, made no mention of the constitutional issue. It did, however, promise a Bill to provide for the valuation of land in England. That promise was repeated by Asquith in May 1908. On 12 February 1908 the Prime Minister spoke for last time in the House of Commons and next day suffered a third heart attack. He continued to govern from No. 10 Downing Street. On 4 March the King visited him at home before he left on holiday in Biarritz. The King would have liked to settle the stewardship of his kingdom before taking his holiday. But he deferred to the Prime Minister's optimism.

His hopes of recovery departed by the end of the month. On 3 April 1908 he tendered his resignation to the King and summoned Asquith. He told him 'You have been a wonderful colleague, so loyal, so disinterested, so able. You are the greatest gentleman I have ever met.'[1] He assured Asquith that he wanted him to succeed. There was no one to compare to Asquith. The King accepted Sir Henry's resignation on 3 April and summoned Asquith to Biarritz. The passing of office gave rise to an acute observation: 'Mr Asquith has not ... the fundamental convictions of his predecessor.'[2]

Edward VII had appointed Herbert Asquith his Prime Minister and First Lord of the Treasury at Hotel du Palais. They adjourned to discuss the composition of the cabinet with him for an hour over breakfast. Asquith would serve nine years in his new position – the longest term since Lord Liverpool in 1827.

C-B stayed on in Downing Street after resigning until his death on 22 April 1908. Churchill immediately commented on his generosity and indulgence

---

[1] J. A. Spender, *The Life of Sir Henry Campbell-Bannerman* vol ii p. 206.
[2] A. G. Gardiner, *Pillars of Society* p. 118.

towards him and said: 'It was only at the end of his life that he emerged into the sunshine – the sunset it was – of popularity, of public affection, to the trust of the House of Commons, and to great political power.'[1] Paying tribute to him in the House of Commons four days later, Asquith said:

[he was] the least cynical of mankind but none had a keener eye for the humour or ironies of the political situation. He was a strenuous and uncompromising fighter, a strong party man, but he harboured no resentment. He met both good and evil fortune with the same unclouded brow, the same unruffled temper, the same unshakeable confidence in the justice and righteousness of his cause. In politics I think he may be fairly described as an idealist in aim, and an optimist by temperament. Great causes appealed to him. He was not ashamed, even on the verge of old age, to see visions and dream dreams

> This man is freed from servile bands
> Of hope to rise and fear to fall;
> Lord of himself, although not of lands;
> And, having nothing, yet hath all.[2]

The verse had been written by Sir Henry Wotton. and on hearing it Sir Henry had asked it to be repeated a few months before.

Asquith had been discussing Cabinet appointments since Edward VII had assured him a month before, on 3 March 1908, at Buckingham Palace that when the Prime Minister resigned he would be asked to take over. Churchill had wanted to remain Under-Secretary for the Colonies, and, yet, sit alongside his Secretary of State in Cabinet. This was reckoned impossible. He was considered for the Admiralty, which he described as 'the most pleasant and glittering' ministerial position. But he declined on personal grounds – his uncle, Lord Tweedmouth, was First Sea Lord. When offered the Local Government Board Churchill refused to consider it. He hated meddlesome detail. He preferred the broader brush, the larger canvas. 'There is no place in the Government more laborious, more anxious, more thankless, more choked with petty and squalid detail, more full of hopeless and insoluble difficulties; . . .'[3] He also told Marsh, 'I refuse to be shut up in a soup kitchen with Mrs Sidney Webb.'[4]

From Biarritz, Asquith offered Churchill a Cabinet seat as President of the Board of Trade with an undertaking to make up the salary to that of a Secretary of State – i.e. £3000 a year. Churchill accepted and thus he took the place of Lloyd George

---

[1] *Glasgow Herald* 23 April 1908.
[2] Hansard vol 89 col 1672–4.
[3] R. Churchill *Winston S. Churchill* vol ii p. 241.
[4] C. Hassal, *Edward Marsh* p. 121.

who moved into Asquith's former post at the Exchequer. Only Lord Elgin was sacked from the previous administration. He went reluctantly and refused a marquisate. Walter Runciman entered the cabinet as President of the Board of Education. He had told Asquith that if Lloyd George was made Chancellor he would not continue as Financial Secretary to the Treasury because 'he does not consider Lloyd-George's personal probity above suspicion, while he knows Lloyd George would sacrifice anyone and allow any amount of suspicion to fall on anyone to save himself, if scandal occurred'.[1]

Campbell-Bannerman often had referred to Asquith's formidable power in mastering a case and debating it with gravitas, and had called him 'the sledge-hammer'. Gladstone did not share that opinion after hearing his maiden speech. 'Too forensic', muttered the Grand Old Man. 'From the first to the last years of his premiership,' wrote one historian, 'he was the giant of the Commons debate.'[2] 'His mind', Churchill wrote, 'opened and shut smoothly and exactly, like the breech of a gun.'[3] Yet, as Balfour observed, 'His lucidity of style is a positive disadvantage when he has nothing to say.'[4]

Asquith's capacity for work was insatiable. His command of the case for free trade and constitutional, legal, social, commercial matters was supported by a considerable arsenal of evidence. Although he could grasp new ideas quickly, he lacked altogether a creative mind outside his fields and relied on Lloyd George and Churchill to devise new major policies in taxation and welfare. Lloyd George told Morley in 1908 that 'Asquith was a man of no initiative, and requires to be briefed . . . He is [a] peculiar man. You drop in a fact – he is not very emotional – but eventually it works like a penny in the slot.'[5]

Churchill realised how best to employ the opportunity to develop his own ideas, which Asquith allowed his Cabinet colleagues. 'A carefully-marshalled argument,' he wrote, 'clearly printed, read by him [Asquith] at his leisure, often won his approval and thereafter commanded his decisive support. His orderly, disciplined mind delighted in reason and design. It was worth while spending many hours to state a case in the most concise and effective manner for the eye of the Prime Minister.'[6]

His handling of the Cabinet was described by Churchill:

In Cabinet he was markedly silent. Indeed he never spoke a word in Council if he could get his way without it. He sat, like the great Judge he was, hearing with trained patience the case deployed on every side, now and then interjecting a question or brief comment, searching or pregnant, which gave matters a turn towards the goal he wished to reach;

[1] B. Murray, *The People's Budget 1909–10* p. 72.
[2] R. C. K. Ensor, *England 1870–1914* p. 407.
[3] WSC, *Great Contemporaries* p .83.
[4] Ibid p. 158.
[5] L. Masterman, *CFG Masterman* p. 137.
[6] WSC, *Great Contemporaries* p. 85.

and when at the end, amidst all the perplexities and vehemently expressed opinion, he summed up, it was very rarely that the silence he had observed till then, did not fall on all.[1]

Asquith's second wife, Margot, was a forceful character. As a young socialite she had been outspoken and yet charming. Sitting next to Lord Randolph Churchill she chided him for resigning as Chancellor more out of temper than on account of conviction. 'Confound your cheek,' exclaimed Lord Randolph. But by the evening's close, he was so disarmed by her that he asked her to dine with a party including the Prince of Wales. She attended in a diaphanous chemise which the other ladies thought outrageous. Their adverse opinion was not, however, shared by the Prince, who invited her to sit at his side and he listened to her complaints of the other female guests.

Though possessed of no academic education, she considered herself intellectually equal to any. She made friends with Benjamin Jowett, the Master of Balliol. Tennyson read her poetry. Gladstone, aged eighty, wrote her a poem and read poetry to her in her bedroom.

She was slow to marry. There were rumours that she was thinking of Balfour. Denying that speculation, Balfour added drily. 'I rather think of having a career of my own.' When she first met Asquith other men appeared to her as so much 'waste paper'. Her opinion was not affected by the fact that he was then married to a wife, who died shortly after the first meeting. She married Asquith afterwards.

She saw politics as more concerned with politicians than with political principles or issues. She had belief in her own judgement and a belief that what was true was incapable of wounding. She sought to protect her husband from the press and opponents with frequent letters filled with underlined emphasis and concluded with the order that they should be burned. Though she sought to shield her husband, she succeeded often in embarrassing him. For she had to explain that she was acting on her own, even when it was reasonable to suspect she was not. Her stepdaughter, Violet, wrote, '[Churchill] neither dazzled nor disarmed her. There was always something a little prickly in their relationship, perhaps because neither of them liked listening.'[2]

It was no wonder that at the age of sixty Asquith fell in love with Venetia Stanley aged twenty-six, nor surprising that his letters to her over a three-year period would have filled three medium-length books.

Churchill formed a particularly close working relationship with Lloyd George. Their styles were quite different. Churchill was moved by ideas and Lloyd George by strategic calculation. He regarded politics more as an art of persuasion. 'He could charm the bark off a tree,' commented Margot Asquith.

---

[1] Ibid.
[2] V. Bonham Carter, *Churchill As I Knew Him*, p. 121.

His friendship with Churchill was not a conventional partnership. Churchill, although born the grandson of a duke, had little regard for conventions or generally approved standards of thought or behaviour. Lloyd George's upbringing had been an altogether different matter. It was described by Churchill. 'The offspring of the Welsh village whose whole youth had been rebellion against the aristocracy, who had skipped indignantly out of the path of the local Tory magnate driving his four-in-hand, and revenging himself at night on the magnate's rabbits.'[1]

Lloyd George was eleven years older. He was a great influence on Churchill, who was content to serve as his political apprentice. Before his meeting in the cabinet with Lloyd George, Churchill had been interested principally in ideas.

Together they forged the foundations of a social policy for this century. They became the engine of Liberal reform. Their ideas were concerned with the mitigation of poverty, while Churchill had formerly been pre-occupied with causes. He was at one with the leading light in cabinet and together they assumed its leadership.

The rest of the cabinet was filled by Victorian men principally. Of these Churchill had a special friendship with Morley, a man of letters. Morley was an idealist. Campbell-Bannerman had called him Priscilla and near his death he referred to Morley as 'a breath of sunshine.'[2] He was an interesting conversationalist. He was, commented J A Spender, 'one of the very few people who seemed to be arguing for truth, not for victory.'[3] Morley said:

> I have a great liking for Winston for his vitality, his indefatigable industry and attention to business, his remarkable gift of language and skill in argument and his curious flair for all sorts of political cases as they arise though even he now and then makes mistakes a pretty bubble for a great wave. All the same as I so often tell him in a paternal way a successful politician in this country needs a good deal more computations of other peoples opinions without anxiety about his own.[4]

Morley had studied the eighteenth-century enlightenment, the early nineteenth-century and had sat at the feet of John Stuart Mill. He hailed the Frenchman Turgot as his ideal philosopher statesman. In the 1870s he was considered a Liberal radical along with Sir Charles Dilke and Chamberlain. He had written a biography of Cobden.

Morley was not against Government doing anything, as Churchill maintained, but he was against state action which was not aimed at effecting causal reform to

---

[1] WSC, *Great Contemporaries* p. 178.
[2] J. A. Spender, *The Life of Sir Henry Campbell-Bannerman* vol ii p. 384.
[3] F. W. Knickerbocker, *John Morley and his Friends* p. 138.
[4] L. Broad, *Winston Churchill* p. 59.

promote a just prosperity. Churchill wrote of his experience of sitting with Morley for six years in Cabinet, 'Six years of constant friendship, to me stimulating propinquity.'[1]

In a conversation with John Morgan several years later Morley remembered Lloyd George. '. . . He has got what Carlyle said of the Hindu god – he has got fire in his belly, but his weakness is looseness of mind.'

Morgan: 'And his principles?'

Morley: 'Principles! Do you talk to me of his principles? What are they? But he is not dishonest, he's only tricky. Some shabbiness perhaps.'[2]

Morley had sat in Campbell-Bannerman's Cabinet as Secretary of State for India but at his request on grounds of health he was sent to the Lords and became Lord Privy Seal under Asquith.

The War Minister, Haldane, was a brilliant lawyer, but an undistinguished advocate before a jury, who expected a more worldly, less intellectual advocate. He elucidated points of law with elegance and clarity before the bench in the Higher Courts. He had been educated in Germany and studied German philosophy. In 1906 he had wanted to be Lord Chancellor, but C-B appointed him Minister of War. 'We shall see', he said, 'how Schopenhauer (as he called him) gets on in the kale yard.' C-B had not trusted him; 'Haldane', he commented, 'is always climbing up and down the backstairs but he makes such a clatter that everyone hears him.'[3] But Haldane mastered his task and reorganised the regular army, still not recovered from the Boer War, saved £2 million per annum in War Office expenditure, created the Territorial Army and delivered a trained and equipped army for the First World War. In short, he proved himself an outstanding Minister of War.

By convention appointment to the Cabinet required a by-election, to give the electorate in the minister's constituency an opportunity to approve that appointment. Churchill's Unionist opponent in Manchester was again Joynson-Hicks. He had been forced into becoming a 'whole-hogger' protectionist; Churchill had described him as a 'mild retaliationist' in his earlier days. Once again free trade was the main issue. 'There are other issues, but', he asked in his Address, 'is there any half so important to Lancashire?' Joynson-Hicks fought a traditional Tory fight; for the Church, beer, the Lords, Tariff Reform, and no doubt for the Union Jack, a customary artefact of popular imperialism at Tory election meetings. This time Churchill was defeated in the poll by 429 votes and by an opponent whom H. G. Wells described as 'an entirely undistinguished man . . . an obscure and ineffectual nobody.'[4]

Later Churchill wrote to the local chairman of the Liberal party. 'But there is in

[1] WSC, *Great Contemporaries* p. 81.
[2] J. Morgan, *John Morley* p. 41.
[3] J. Wilson *CB A Life of Sir Henry Campdell-Bannerman* p. 145.
[4] R. Churchill, *Winston S. Churchill* vol ii p. 235.

the heart of every political reverse the dynamic impulse of a future triumph. You must turn the emotion of defeat to the process of recovery, so that the very hour of disaster becomes the seed-time of victory ... although my Parliamentary connection with the division has now terminated I shall consider myself under special obligations to help so far as my strength permits me to defend Free Trade in the great City to whose prosperity and fame Free Trade is vital.'[1] It was no hollow undertaking.

'The belief among competent observers', wrote Morley, 'is that the resounding defeat of Winston at Manchester was due to wrath at rather too naked tactics of making deals with this and that and the other groups without too severe a scrutiny in his own political conscience of the terms they were exacting from him. In other words Winston has no principles. It is believed that he lost 300–400 of these honourably fastidious electors.' Morley added. 'I have a great liking for Winston; for his vitality, his remarkable gift of language and skill in argument, and his curious flair for all sorts of political cases as they arise, though even he now and then mistakes a frothy bubble for a great wave.'[2]

The London Stock Exchange sent a telegram to the defeated minister. It read, 'What's the use of a W.C. without a seat?' Other telegrams arrived offering him 'eight or nine' constituencies. After the poll Churchill walked the 300-yard distance from the Town Hall in Manchester to the Reform Club where a telegram from the Liberal Party of Dundee awaited him, offering him their candidacy. The Prime Minister later confirmed Churchill's decision to fight that seat.

He won the by-election comfortably in Dundee on 9 May 1908. His speeches in Dundee were reported in the national press. He was in a strong position. He could claim that bills on temperance, education, lower hours in coal mining, land tenure and land taxation had been drawn up. John Morley wrote to congratulate him. 'I thought your first speech one of the ablest and most effective I have read for many a day'.[3]

He took his place in cabinet. He married Clementine Hozier, daughter of Lady Blanche Hozier, who was herself daughter of the seventh Earl of Airlie. He had never been a lady's man. The few parties he had attended he had spent talking to the married women. On his second meeting Churchill asked Clementine whether she read his biography of his father. When she replied negatively, he assured her that it would be sent round to her next morning in a hansom. She was disappointed when he did not. Churchill revealed his lively sense of fun to in a letter to her in August 1908, in which he recounted a fire in a house he was staying for the wedding of his brother Jack. He took over charge of directing the rescue operation. He asked Clementine to Blenheim Palace. The weekend might have passed unremarkably but a shower of rain forced them to take cover in a

---

[1] Chartwell Papers 4/7 23.
[2] J. Morley, *Recollections* vol. 2 p. 255.
[3] Chartwell Papers 4/19 22.

summer house. There Winston stammered out his proposal, which was accepted. On the day of his wedding in early September the *Tailor and Cutter* observed critically that Churchill's wedding suit was 'one of the greatest failures as a wedding garment we have ever seen', causing him to have a 'glorified coachman appearance'. There was a cartoon of Churchill holding a stocking, with a grin, over the caption: *Winston's Latest Line – Hoziery*. Lloyd George told that, even amid the fuss Churchill remained with his feet on the ground and that in the registry at the marriage service, Churchill discussed politics. 'I married', wrote Churchill, 'and lived happily ever afterwards.' Prior to this, he was not interested in acquiring female friendship, unless they became as interested as he in his political life. He had not been keen on dancing parties, or treading a social catwalk outside politics.

Churchill arrived at the Board of Trade and observed, 'I have got to this pie too late; Lloyd George has pulled out all the plums.' Lloyd George had delivered the Patent & Design Act and the Merchant Shipping Act. He left him only the Port of London Bill then before Parliament. Detailed and major measures these might have been, but no delicacies to be sure. Churchill took over the Miners' Eight Hour Bill from the Home Secretary. This was the first measure to limit a man's working hours. Though the cost was estimated at 26 million tons per annum, it afforded Churchill an excellent opportunity to champion the cause of the subterranean workers. Miners, he said, needed leisure to see their homes, their wives and their children in daylight. They needed time to think, to read and to cultivate their gardens. Later in the session he supported a Member's Bill to create summertime, which lengthened the daylight hours. The Bill was resisted in the Lords who had more regard to the recipients of mining royalties than the subterranean workers. They mutilated the Bill.

In 1908 he had to conciliate industrial disputes, of which there were more than in any previous year to 1892. He conciliated the engineers, the shipbuilders who were faced by a lock-out, and the cotton workers. He set up a permanent Court of Arbitration.

The new Government approached their legislative programme cautiously. Asquith had none of the radical fervour of his predecessor and none of his vision. He cared for the parliamentary and constitutional institutions like a curator cares for treasures entrusted to him.

Asquith presented the 1908 Budget himself, although he had become Prime Minister. Its main feature was the introduction of pensions, payable in accordance with provisions of the Old Age Peoples Act 1908. It was payable from I January in 1909 to the over-seventies and earning less than £26, or £39 (both per annum) for married couples – thought to number 1.2 million – at a rate of 5s for single and 7s 6d per week respectively. Criminals, loafers, lunatics and those in receiving poor law relief were not eligible. The Bill passed the Lords in June only because they did not want to anger Labour supporters, by being seen to oppose it. 'This measure, I am much afraid', intoned Lord Lansdowne magisterially, 'is one which will weaken the moral fibre of the nation and diminish the self-respect of our people.'[1] They amended the Bill to give expression to their grave unease. But the Commons rejected them and, when the Government pointed out that it was a money Bill, their Bill went through.

Churchill asked the electorate to see through the hypocrisy of Lord Lansdowne and his ennobled fellows.

> You will observe that in Lord Lansdowne's opinion, the workhouse was the only method by which the self-respect of our people could be maintained; but, although Lord Lansdowne took such strong action about the . . . Act, although his friends and supporters used even stronger language than he, they passed it, although they thought it would demoralise the country and sap the self-respect of our nation – they passed it. They thought it was not good ground to fight on.[2]

One may note a profound step in political action. The Government was embarking for the first time on social expenditure. Previously people who had led active lives either retired into poverty or continued work in order to exist until death. Before the concept of a state pension is accepted as a social institution of this century, one might ask why the mass of the people lived in the shadow of poverty and were not able to provide for their retirement. It is difficult to disagree with the basic questions and answers supplied by Philip Snowden during the Third Reading in the Commons.

> I ask: What is the justification of a scheme for old age pensions at all? I think the only justification for old age pensions is that there are people who need provision for old age. But then comes the further question: Why are people in this condition? Why are they poor after a hard-working life of fifty or sixty years? They are poor and they are dependent on some form of support in old age for the simple reason that, notwithstanding their hard work, they have not been able out of the income they have received to make provision for old age.[3]

To point to the evident problem of poverty in old age and attempt to solve it through increased taxation, necessary to finance pensions, is simplistic.

Churchill delivered in June 1908 some robust thoughts on taxation, which merit inscription in gold lettering wherever men deliberate state expenditure.

---

[1] Hansard [Lords] vol 192 col 1417.
[2] WSC, *The People's Rights* 1970 edn p. 32.
[3] Hansard vol 192 cols 148–9.

Herbert Asquith

Churchill and Lloyd George

Churchill and his wife

Churchill as First Lord of the Admiralty

Taxation, raise it as you please, is a gross and unredeemable evil, [he growled] . . . All taxation is an evil a necessary evil, if you will, but still an evil, in so far as taxation is concerned, harsh, unmingled, and unmitigated . . . When the state takes arbitrarily from the savings or earnings of the people sums of money, great or small, it withdraws that money from the healthy fructifications of industry and trade and it diminishes – cannot fail to diminish – the consuming & productive energies of the people.[1]

The real issue for the House of Commons when dealing with poverty in old age was to eliminate the cause of poverty in society, which prevented an individual looking after himself or herself in old age. Snowden was right to draw attention to the cause of poverty and Churchill was right to deride taxation as an unnecessary curse.

Having seen the Budget pass both houses of parliament, the government sought to challenge the Lords over the unsolved problem of liquor licensing. In June 1906 Churchill had mused about the pretensions of the Upper House,

He did not want to quarrel with the House of Lords [it was reported] He admired the way they looked after their own interests and regarded their own property, and the versatility of character, which enabled them on one day to pose as the champions of the spiritual needs of children and on the next as the champions of the spirituous needs of the brewers. When he saw the great and noble Liberal majority which had been returned, it reminded him of a steamroller: it worked without hurry, it worked steadily on its course, grinding all the roughness out.

The education question was still unresolved. Nonconformists objected to their children being fed the Anglican doctrine at public expense funded from the rates and the Anglicans insisted that they were paying local rates to have their children raised like themselves, not like the Nonconformists. The first Education Bill sought to replace the support of schools from the local rates and transfer them to national taxation. In other words, move the control of education from local authorities to Parliament. The Bill met much hostility from both sides. The Bishop of Manchester spoke for one side by muttering, what sounded like the last rites of the measure, that it was 'a specimen of class legislation, of unscrupulous rapacity, and of religious intolerance in the twentieth century, the Bill would deserve a place in historical archives by the side of racks, thumbscrews, boots and other engines of torture'.[2]

After its First Reading it was dropped. Asquith held talks with Davidson, the

---

[1] *Times* 26 June 1908.
[2] C. Cross, *Liberals in Power* p. 71.

Archbishop of Canterbury, to discuss an an alternative measure. A more moderate Bill was agreed, whereby denominational teaching could be given for two days each week at the expense of the denomination. However the archbishop was not supported by his bishops, who condemned the measure. Like the earlier attempt it was withdrawn.[1]

By way of illustration of the robustness of political thought before the First War, the spirit of an elderly minister in Asquith's Government merits mention. In August 1908 religious difficulties erupted over a proposed march of the Catholic Blessed Sacrament in central London. The Protestant Alliance protested. The Home Secretary sensed danger and wanted the Catholics to call off their march. Asquith asked the Lord Privy Seal, Lord Ripon, to use his influence with the Catholic hierarchy, whom he knew well. Lord Ripon, aged eighty-one, was able to bring about the Prime Minister's intent but he resigned from the Cabinet in September to protest at the Government's attempt to stifle religious activity. Two months later he was the guest at the Eighty Club, which was a dining club. Replying to a friendly tribute from Asquith, he proudly stated, 'I started at the high level of radicalism and in 1852 I was considered to be a dangerous young man. I am a Radical still, just as much as then, but I am much more respectable.'[2] He had been Viceroy in India, Leader of the House of Lords and elder statesman. Success in office like this normally removes every trace of the radical spirit.

Churchill and Lloyd George were committed to social reform; to expensive measures such as pensions, labour exchanges, national insurance and unemployment insurance. That priority had been contained in the Liberal election manifesto. They were keen to restrain military expenditure. Churchill had a tradition inherited from his father against military expenditure. Lloyd George questioned military expenditure and Churchill, with his military experience, acted like his financial ferret. Looking back on his partnership Churchill described his relationship in more formal terms, 'I was his lieutenant . . .'[3] Asquith allowed a debate on military expenditure to range unrestrained in Cabinet. In fact Churchill was allowed access to War Office files and was given his own room in that Ministry.

Haldane was a considerable opponent for Churchill to take on over the question of military expenditure. Churchill delivered a report to cabinet. He argued there was too much expense in the War Office and too little on the field of battle. Haldane wrote a memorandum which devastated Churchill's argument.

The attention of the Chancellor of the Exchequer and his lieutenant then turned to naval expenditure. The First Sea Lord, Fisher, maintained that naval power had long been the first line of defence and it had reigned supreme. In 1905/6 he built and launched a new order of battleship – the dreadnought which

---

[1] The demands of religion and education were fused finally in Butler's Education Act 1944.
[2] *Times*, 25 Nov 1908.
[3] Hansard, 28 March 1945.

was armed with ten 12-inch guns, eight of which could be brought to bear on the same target in almost every direction. The dreadnought bore this massive armoury at a speed of three knots faster than any battleship afloat and it had twice the firing power normally mounted on a battleship. Its introduction effectively rendered existing battleships obsolete. It afforded an opportunity for other navies to build smaller but more modern forces.

When the Liberals came to power in 1906 they reduced the British battleship building programme up to 1908 from 16 to 12. In 1906 Germany laid the keel of the first dreadnought. In 1907 the keels of another three dreadnoughts were laid down in shipyards. In April 1908 the Reichstag passed a Naval Law, which authorised the construction of four new dreadnoughts and in the following year four more. Upon completion of the building of the programme up to 1909, which was scheduled for 1912 Germany would have 13 and Britain 16. This was not the margin of superiority which pleased the Admiralty. As events unfurled it appeared that the Germans were acting in advance of their programme and completing much sooner than had been allowed.

Fisher could not have had a better cue for arguing the case of increasing naval power than Germany's naval programme. He had viewed the new German navy with hostility. At the end of 1908 Britain had 43 battleships which had been built before the advent of the dreadnought and Germany 22. Britain had two dreadnoughts and Germany none. He was given, instead of an agreed four, six dreadnoughts – super dreadnoughts – on an annual basis.

But Lloyd George and Churchill wanted the programme to be reduced to four. In the summer they made public speeches to the effect that Germany had no reason and no place to fight. Fisher had been leaking estimates and cabinet discussions to Garvin, the editor of the *Observer*. He wanted eight in place of the six. The debate came alive in the winter of 1908/9 when the 1909 naval estimates were due to be published. The cry of Unionists, 'We want Eight and we won't wait', was taken up. But the pressure within the cabinet was Asquith's main worry. For the first time he complained of Winston; he had expected this from Lloyd George. 'I am afraid Winston is proving himself to be thoroughly untrustworthy.[1] Asquith might well have agreed with one of Lloyd-George's insights into Churchill's character, when he compared him to 'a chauffeur who apparently perfectly sane and drives with great skill for months, then suddenly takes you over a precipice.'[2] Lloyd George and Churchill were determined either to win a reduction to four or to resign. This might have been a general criticism for it was evident in several fields; yet it had only surfaced in this naval dispute. McKenna and Fisher wanted at least six in order to remain at the Admiralty and they were supported in cabinet by Grey, Runciman and Haldane. Lloyd George and

---

[1] V. Bonham Carter, *Churchill As I Knew Him* p. 169.
[2] T. Jones, *Diary* 8 June 1922.

Churchill relied on Morley, Loreburn, Burns and Harcourt. In February 1909 Asquith announced a compromise which both sides accepted. There would be four and four more in the following year, and work would begin in the next financial year on the second four, if it was proved they were needed.

Churchill commented in his book, *World Crisis*. 'A curious and characteristic solution was reached. The Admiralty had demanded six ships: the economists offered four and we finally compromised on eight.' He also conceded that: 'Although the Chancellor and I were right in the narrow sense we were absolutely wrong in relation to the deep tides of destiny. The greatest credit is due to the First Lord of the Admiralty for the resolute and courageous manner in which he fought his case and withstood his Party on this occasion.'[1] A conclusion of this affair seems to have been Asquith's opinion, which he told Lord Crewe, was that 'Lloyd George has no principles and Winston no convictions.'[2]

At Dundee Churchill spoke of the grand reforms which he and Lloyd George had been dreaming and devising:

> I feel and I dare say you feel to, that we have reached a climacteric in the life of this Parliament. The next six months will probably determine the whole remaining fortunes of the Government, and decide whether a gradual but progressive decline will slowly carry the Administration in the natural course to the grave where so many others are peacefully slumbering, or whether, deriving fresh vigour from its exertions, it will march forward to conquer.

The main business in 1908 was the Licensing Bill. The Government saw alcohol as a source of poverty and misery but the Unionists in both Houses believed that beer as a source of merriment and profit. The odd excess was unfortunate, they might admit, but a small price for what the Romans called 'bread and circuses', meaning a device to keep the lower orders from thinking too seriously of sober realities. Much as he hated intemperance then, Churchill was sensitive to framing a law to rid society of it. He did not want to set the conditions for the exercise of the individual's freedom to drink as he wished. The main aim of the Bill was to close 32,000 public houses – a third of the total in England and Wales – over a period of fourteen years. So the number of public houses would be linked to population. Compensation was to be offered, not from public sources, but from a levy among brewers. Churchill questioned the need of the Lords deciding this question on behalf of the people.

> It would be a great thing', he affirmed, 'to have expected the Lords to allow the people to settle for themselves, you would think it would be

---

[1] WSC *World Crisis 1911–14* pp. 36–8.
[2] R. Churchill, *Winston S. Churchill* vol ii p. 247.

the conditions upon which the sale of intoxicating liquors should be sold in their own neighbourhoods. Each district has to pay for the expense of disease, crime, misery and destitution which follows from the excessive use of alcohol. . . . And yet upon purely tactical grounds – because it was important to the Unionist Party to keep the public house vote – in spite of the advice of middle-minded men, in spite of the appeals of the Bishops of the Church – to their honour – and the Archbishop of Canterbury, the House of Lords cast away this Bill upon which the whole labour of the House of Commons had been spent; and by that act sent a message of despair to every social worker, to every philanthropic body, to every Christian minister, to every little Sunday school throughout the land.[1]

Speaking in the Commons during the Second Reading, Asquith explained the two aims of the Bill, which had been drafted in the main by him. First, to improve the conditions in which the liquor trade was carried on. This would be done by reducing the number of liquor licenses and by other secondary measures. 'There is a relation', he argued, 'between temptation and excess, between the growth and exercise of this pernicious habit and the invitation and opportunity held out for its indulgence'. Second, to recover to the State dominion and control of this monopoly.

At one public meeting Asquith delivered a typical speech on the measure which had been largely drafted by himself. His speech was packed with statistics and trade details. With admiration of his statistical presentation, a lady came to the platform at the end of the meeting and wondered whether she could keep the Prime Minister's notes as a souvenir. He handed the one paper which had been his entire notes. On it were written three words: 'Too many pubs'.[2]

The decisive rejection of the Licensing Bill in November 1908 by the House of Lords – by voting 272 votes to 96 – revived the question of the House of Lords' veto. 'It was rejected', said Asquith in Southport on 2 July 1909, 'without even any pretence of consideration of its details, it was rejected in pursuance of a pre-concerted party resolution, it was rejected with every circumstance of contumely and contempt.' It ended a bad year for the Government. The landslide of 1906 seemed to have slipped away. They had been defeated in six by-elections and seen their majorities fall in six others. '[Churchill] was perfectly furious at the rejection of Licensing Bill by the Lords, stabbed at his bread, would hardly speak: murmured perorations about "the heart of every Band of Hope in this country sinking within them". We shall send them such a Budget as shall terrify them, they have started a class war, they had better be careful.'[3] He admitted in a letter

---

[1] WSC, *The People's Rights* 1970 edn p. 3.
[2] C. Cross, *Liberals in Power*, C Cross p. 70.
[3] L. Masterman, *C F G Masterman*, p. 114.

to Hugh Massingham in January 1909: 'The Licensing Bill was unpopular throughout English constituencies, and the Lords who always act upon excellent caucus information, gained strength by rejecting it.'

The problem of introducing a bill to tax land value was unresolved. The Lords simply rejected any such measure. This was one measure in the Government's legislation which could be included in a money bill. Without a valuation no taxation could be imposed; it was the first step. In December 1908 Josiah Wedgwood presented a petition to the Prime Minister signed by 246 MPs. It consisted of one sentence: The signatories 'respectfully urge upon the Government the desirability of including a Tax on Land Values in next year's Budget.' It was felt that the Lords would not dare to reject a Budget.

7

The Untrodden Field

When land value taxation was popular during the premiership of Campbell-Bannerman, Churchill became its leading light. The advocates of this policy believed that taxation of land value would destroy the unjust distribution of wealth and remove the cause of poverty. Furthermore, the taxation of land value would confine taxation to public property and there would be no reason for the taxation to spread on private property.

When welfare provision became prominent under the less radical leadership of Asquith, Churchill soon assumed, along with Lloyd George, the role of its principal spokesmen. This policy amounted to leaving poverty's underlying cause undisturbed and attempting to mitigate its effects.

Politicians deluded themselves and the electorate that the state could look after able-bodied men and women who were unable to look after themselves. The immediate political question is: what is the cause of an able-bodied individual in a democracy being unable to look after himself. The question of general mitigation of poverty is a secondary question, which arises, if at all, when the primary question has been acknowledged and addressed. Churchill, however, answered the first in the clearest terms. He argued that land value was created by society, that it constituted public property. It cannot be seriously argued that Churchill was in any doubt as to what the taxation of land value would achieve. Therefore, the second question regarding the provision of welfare did not need addressing by Churchill himself.

Asquith could be expected to be led down the road of mitigation. For he had little political imagination and no creative political powers. Lloyd George had no principles and every question was like putty in his hands. But Churchill was not of the same mould of plasticity. He possessed oratory, charisma, political intelligence and a grand vision. He had written to Asquith shortly before his appointment to the Cabinet in April 1908 that:

'Dimly across gulfs of ignorance I see the outline of a policy wh I call the Minimum Standard . . . I am doubtful of my power to give it concrete expression. If I did, I expect before long I should find myself in collision with some of my best friends – like for instance Morley, who at the end of a lifetime of study &

thought has come to the conclusion that nothing can be done.'[1] Masterman felt that Churchill 'was full of the poor whom he had just discovered. He thinks he is called by providence – to do something for them. "Why have I always been kept safe within a hair's breath except to do something like this?" '[2]

Churchill gave entirely the wrong impression of Morley's thinking. Morley believed that if Government reformed the causes of poverty, it need not trouble itself with mitigating its effects. In other words, if a leaking pipe is repaired, the bucket and sponge are no longer required. Churchill did not appreciate the distinction between reforming the cause and mitigating the effects of an unreformed cause. He championed radical steps to alter the distribution of wealth through the taxation of land values and understood that this policy would attack the root of poverty. Yet he also embraced with equal enthusiasm measures to mitigate unrelieved poverty. He did not admit that mitigation at public expense was bound to exacerbate the condition of poverty, as it would demand increased taxation. He did not understand that the existing form of taxation, which fell on personal wealth, intensified the cause of poverty.

Churchill's interest in the mitigation of poverty went back several years. He came to regard this area of Government policy as the untrodden field of politics. He had been introduced by Morley, in December 1901, to a study of poverty, which had been published earlier that year – Seebolm Rowntree's *Poverty: A Study Of Town Life*. Reading the book made a vivid impression on him. The author showed in 400 pages of details and tables that 27.8 per cent of the 46,000 population of York were living in poverty compared with Charles Booth's estimate in London that 30 per cent of the metropolitan population lived in poverty. Both books showed poverty was more serious than generally supposed. In an unpublished review of *Poverty: A Study of Town Life*, which Churchill had written in 1902, Churchill had praised the patient endeavours of Mr Rowntree.

In effect, he had posed a question which lay at the heart of Victorian society: what was the cause of poverty? Yet his research had been directed only to the patterns and appearances of poverty. It appeared to him as a problem that had something to do with alcohol abuse, low wages, defective housing, poor education, lack of self-reliance and self-discipline. Indeed his statistical survey, despite its detail and precision, was an inconclusive document. For alcoholism, poor education, squalid housing, irresponsibility by parents were manifestations of general poverty, the cause of which he failed to identify.

Churchill wrote that, 'the imagination was not stirred by the slum, the garret, and the gutter.' Nevertheless he drew a penetrating conclusion. 'Consider the peculiar case of these poor and the consequences. Although the British Empire is so large that they cannot find room to live in it; although it is so magnificent,

---

[1] R. Churchill, *Winston S. Churchill* vol ii p. 242–3.
[2] L .Masterman, *CF Masterman* p. 97.

they would have had a better chance of happiness if they had been born cannibal islanders of the Southern seas; although its science is so profound, they would have been more healthy if they had been subjects of Hardicanute.'[1] Nineteenth-century political thought had supplied no answer to the poverty which had existed for many centuries. Not only had poverty been allowed to continue but, with time, intensify. It was harshly stigmatised as evidence of moral infirmity and it was seen as an individual problem. In the past it had been attributed to individual weaknesses which could be remedied by the stocks, banishment, transportation or by the workhouse The poor law administration, along with its moral righteousness and starch-collared Guardians, were seen to be incompetent.

It was not the widening of the franchise throughout the nineteenth century, or the growth in urban and rural poverty which accompanied the industrial progress, or the violence which protesters against unemployment showed themselves capable of inflicting on society, or the rise of the Labour Party which made poverty a topical question – it was the Boer War which really brought home the extent of poverty in Britain. Asquith admitted that poverty was more extensive than ever imagined. 'What', he questioned, 'is the use of talking of Empire if here, at its very centre, there is always to be found a mass of people, stunted in education, prey to intemperance, huddled and congested beyond the possibility of realising in any true sense either social or domestic life?'[2] The report of the Inspector-General of Recruiting initiated a public debate on the health of children and cast such doubt on the unregulated system that demands for state intervention became inevitable.

Considerable expenditure could be allocated to alleviate the various manifestations of poverty. But the expenditure had to be funded from taxpayers. The greater proportion of tax was collected from the poor, who comprised a much larger number than did the rich. Thus particular ills could be remedied by mitigation, but only at the cost of greater general poverty and unemployment.

Rowntree's argument delighted the Webbs, the celebrated sociological engineers, and many other folk who were minded to eradicate poverty. For mitigation promised to be an endless labour and it engendered many more social problems than it could ever solve; it offered the prospect of greater employment, the compilation of volumes of details and statistics, an increase of sentimental compassion – in short, a task which would occupy bureaucracy through eternity. The concentration on mitigation gave rise to that insipid sentimentality which was so much a feature of the Victorian age.

Beatrice Webb had met Churchill in July 1903 and recorded this entry in her diary:

We went into dinner with Winston Churchill. First impression: restless –

---

[1] R. Churchill, *Winston S. Churchill* vol ii p. 31.
[2] B.B. Gilbert, *The Evolution of National Insurance* [1966] p. 77.

almost intolerably so, without capacity for sustained and unexciting labour – egotistical, bumptious, shallow-minded and reactionary, but with a certain personal magnetism, great pluck and some originality – not of intellect but of character. More of an American speculator than an English aristocrat.[1]

Now, however, he was in Cabinet and in search of advice to give form to his perception of social policy. On another occasion, in the spring of 1908, she wrote , 'Winston Churchill dined with us last night . . . we talked exclusively shop. He had swallowed whole Sidney's [her husband] scheme for boy labour and unemployment.'[2]

The Webbs were prominent in the first decade of this century. They held a position in society of unofficial philosophers of social policy. In 1905 Beatrice Webb had been appointed to the Royal Commission on the Poor Law. They were the pioneers of statistical bureaucracy. Their ideas were developed at the end of the Second World War by William Beveridge, their choice disciple, whose Report hastened the move to state regulation. The Webbs eventually allied themselves to the Labour Party in 1914.

Sidney Webb informed Churchill of the progress of the Royal Commission, on which his wife sat. Originally it was intended that the Commission should be concerned with the administration of the Poor Law Guardians. But his wife and Lansbury had managed to extend its outlook to the whole field of social policy. In late 1908 he lent Churchill the draft of the minority report which he had written himself. He also convinced Churchill to accept his ideas for minimum wages and for labour exchanges.

The ramshackle system of the poor law was reviewed by a Royal Commission, appointed in 1905 by Balfour. It reported in 1909 and the majority report of fourteen members of the Commission made unremarkable recommendations concerned with the administration of the poor law regime and the minority report written by Webb and signed by his wife, George Lansbury and two other members recommended taking its administration out of the hands of the Poor Law Guardians and handing it over to local authorities. John Burns, the Minister of the Local Government Board, declined to accept either report and they were shelved along with forty volumes of evidence submitted to the Commission by 1300 witnesses.

The Unemployed Workmen's Act 1905 had been a cautious provision. It established Distress Committees in boroughs over 50,000 but the powers given to them were investigatory. These Committees might dole out sympathy and even money by the handful. But when the cause of unemployment lay unreformed this charity was useless.

---

[1] B Webb, *Our Partnership* pp. 269–70.
[2] Ibid p. 404.

The Liberal Government in 1906 took over a Labour Member's bill to provide school meals at elementary schools, not because they believed in it, but because they did not want to be seen not to. There was, naturally, provision for recovery of the cost from parents. A small measure in itself, but an example of one of the leading nostrums behind so much social policy. The state should, it was generally assumed, enforce a minimum standard, in this case of diet, which the poorer individual parent might choose to do without. The state should look at the causes of the poverty of the parent, but it chose instead to assume the role of a parent.

There is no doubting Churchill's horror at the content of Rowntree's report. His generous nature was affronted. Yet by 1906 he had mastered the argument about the causes of poverty. He had studied the work of George's *Progress and Poverty* which had enjoyed considerable circulation in Britain during the 1880s and 1890s and which had been published internationally.

Churchill agreed with George's diagnosis of the cause and the remedy. George set out to establish that poverty was not a natural condition of society and he demonstrated that it was caused, not by nature, but by human laws. He was not troubled about the intention or the detailed argument of the mitigation of poverty. He had a broader vision and identified the cause.

Indeed Churchill had been so impressed by George as to acknowledge that his conclusions were irrefutable. If these had been ambiguous or unclear in the slightest degree it would be simple to exaggerate their claim to attention. George hated imprecision in language. Their reasoning and exposition were both driven by a relentless determination to pursue an argument or principle to its conclusion. All was light; there were no shadows or dark corners in their arguments.

The main theme in George's work was that only measures to restore justice to the distribution of wealth would remedy poverty. He identified an unjust distribution of wealth as the mother of material, intellectual and spiritual poverty. Poverty might manifest itself in many ways and if separate ministries were formed for each one, government would merely treat the effects rather than the cause : an unjust distribution of wealth. That fact must have been plain from reading *Progress and Poverty* and plain beyond doubt for a thorough student as Churchill.

The consequences of attempting to remedy the different aspects of poverty was to bring into government ministers without real portfolios, thus to open public administration to millions of bureaucrats and to burden the people, and the poor particularly, with taxation that would exacerbate their general poverty. The people may go about with state spectacles and state dentures, but they may be made unemployed by the taxation required to pay for these things. Whereas the individual can take steps to remedy poor eyesight and poor teeth, he cannot overcome the condition of poverty himself.

The taxation of land value was central to George's thinking. He regarded poverty as an unnatural condition which could be remedied only by complying with Nature. He never imagined that it could be solved by more bureaucrats or more rules or more expenditure. Were taxation imposed justly, however, he wrote, 'Men would worry no more about finding employment than they worry about finding air to breathe; they would have no more care about physical necessities than do the lilies of the field.'[1]

Churchill fully appreciated the scale of the argument and the eradication of the causes of poverty. Yet few shared his view. While at the Board of Trade, he devised some policies which savoured more of political expediency than of grand reform. For to prefer mitigation of effects rather than pursue the eradication of causes is to make a weak choice. Removal of the cause is the most effective removal of the effects. Mitigation which leaves the causes undisturbed actually multiplies the effects.

Comparing Socialism with Liberalism in a speech in Glasgow during October 1906 Churchill voiced the outline of his social policy:

> We want to draw a line below which we will not allow persons to live and labour, yet above which they may compete with all the strength of their manhood. We want to have free competition upwards; we decline to allow free competition to run downwards. We do not want to pull down the structures of science and civilisation: but to spread a net over the abyss.

Though these words may have been fine-sounding, they were empty of meaning. Does the establishment of a minimum standard of living by law alter the natural laws governing the distribution of wealth?

Churchill was drawn to consider matters that lay outside his departmental responsibilities at the Board of Trade. He had already made friends with the Webbs. They had advised Balfour and now they realised that Churchill was prepared to come to their frugal soirées and imbibe their social wisdom. Mrs Webb confessed her embarrassment, as the demand for their advice was sought on a personal basis from politicians, across the parties, who were in search of ideas and policies.

Lloyd George looked to Germany which had a system of public insurance for health, unemployment and also labour exchanges. Lloyd George admired these institutions in Germany during a short trip in August 1908. He came to share Churchill's dream of social welfare.

Churchill unfolded the campaign against poverty in Dundee on 9 October 1908. He believed the government

> had opened a door [old age pensions] which will not soon or easily be closed. The Members of both Houses of Parliament have been led to the

---

[1] H. George, *Progress and Poverty* p. 461.

verge of the cruel abyss of poverty and have in solemn session assembled to contemplate its depth and gloom. All alike have come to gaze – none have been unmoved. There are some distinguished and eminent men, who have started back appalled by what they have seen, and whose only idea is to slam the door on the grim and painful prospect which has been revealed to their eyes ... Yes in this famous land of ours, so often the envy of foreigners, where the grace and ease of life have been carried to such perfection, where there is so little class hatred and jealousy, where there is a wide store of political experience and knowledge, where there are such enormous moral forces available, so much wisdom, so much virtue, so much power, we have not yet succeeded in providing that necessary apparatus and security, without which our industrial system is not merely incomplete, but actually inhumane.

Churchill attributed three conditions which made Britain weak in international trade. First, a lack of central control of industry, government work or special relief work.

It would be possible for the Board of Trade to foretell with a certain amount of accuracy the degree of unemployment to be reached in any winter. It ought to be possible for some authority in some government office – which I do not care – to view the whole situation in advance, and within certain limits to exert a powerful influence over the general distribution of Government contracts.

There is nothing economically unsound in increasing temporarily and artificially the demand for labour during a period of temporary and artificial contraction.

Churchill advocated a need to have in 'permanent existence certain recognised industries of a useful but uncompetitive character, like afforestation, managed by public departments and capable of being expanded or contracted according to the needs of the labour market, just as easily as you can pull out the stops or pedals of an organ.'

Secondly, he highlighted the plight of the casual unskilled labour 'whose whole life and the lives of wife and children are embarked in a sort of blind, desperate, fatalistic gamble with circumstances beyond his comprehension and control.' If a man or women could enjoy under a just distribution of wealth the fruits of their labour, could they not acquire skills as they wished?

Third, he drew attention to boy labour:

The whole underside of the labour market is deranged by the competition of boys or young persons who do men's work for boy's wages, and are turned off as soon as they demand men's wages for themselves. That is the evil so far as it affects the men; but how does it affect the boys, the youth of our country, the heirs of all our exertion, the inheritors of that long treasure of history and romance, of science and knowledge – aye, of national glory, for which many valiant generations have fought and toiled – the youth of Britain, how are we treating them in the twentieth century of the Christian era? Are they not being exploited? Are they not being thrown away?'

Child labour is an effect of the deeper cause of poverty in society. It was fanciful to imagine that the problem could be solved by a law forbidding the employment of child labour. Better to allow the level of earnings to rise from levels of basic existence to levels more closely related to individual production.

He left his audience with a vague notion that the rich would feel such a momentous programme would be in their interest to finance. Cobden had warned the House of Commons in the mid-nineteenth century that it was not their business to hand out charity to an entire nation. 'We often hear a great deal about charity, but what have we to do with charity? Yes, I say, what have we to do with charity in this House? The people ask for justice and not charity. We are bound to deal out justice; how can charity be dealt out to an entire nation? Were the nation the recipients, it is difficult to imagine, who would be the donors.'[1]

If politicians would spend as much thought on the raising of revenue as enthusing on the benefits of public expenditure, they would realise how futile it is to pursue a just distribution of wealth through welfare, rather than through justice and freedom.

'Soon, very soon', Churchill concluded, 'our brief lives will be lived. Soon, very soon, we and our affairs will have passed away. Uncounted generations will trample heedlessly upon our tombs. What is the use of living, if it be not to strive for noble causes and to make this muddled world a better place for those who live in it after we are gone? How else can we put ourselves in harmonious relation with the great verities and consolations of the infinite and eternal?'[2]

Churchill's social programme had three main features: legislation for sweated labour, the creation of labour exchanges and insurance for unemployment. The details can be summarised briefly.

He introduced a Trades Board Act in April 1909. Initially it covered 200,000 workers, of whom 140,000 were women and children. A Board was appointed for each trade; with equal representation from the employers and employees, together with outsiders. It set rates of minimum pay.

It was, however, the 'schemes for compulsory unemployment insurance and for the allied labour exchanges [which] were probably Churchill's greatest

---

[1] *Hansard*, 15 May 1843.LXIX col 400.
[2] *Times*, 10 October 1908.

achievement at the Board of Trade. It ensured for him a place among the architects, if only of the foundations, of the modern welfare state. Labour exchanges were an idea promulgated by the Webbs. They would advertise vacancies for unemployed people. Not only did they convert Churchill to their thinking, but they persuaded him to recruit one of their disciples, Beveridge, a twenty-nine year-old Oxford don, to oversee their creation. He could already call on the help of Sir Hubert Lewellyn, his Permanent Secretary.

The Labour Exchange Bill was introduced on its own in May 1909, as recommended by the minority report of the Royal Commission on the Poor Law. Burns, the President of the Local Government Board, had already rejected the reports and, accordingly, was not very sympathetic to Churchill's bill. The country was divided into ten districts. Each was with a divisional chief and a divisional clearing house and they were all subject to national control from Whitehall.

In the autumn of 1909 Churchill visited Germany and was thrilled to see labour exchanges in operation. He could not contain his excitement at introducing them to Britain. On 28 December 1909 he told the electors in Dundee that, '... there was not one of them among the forty or fifty I questioned who had not in his pocket an insurance card stamped and in order, which entitled him to benefit in sickness, in invalidity, in infirmity, or old age.' The first exchanges were opened on 1 February 1910. By the time Lloyd George introduced his National Insurance Act in 1911 there were 414 exchanges open.

The insurance against unemployment became Part 2 of Lloyd George's 1911 Act. It covered about 3 million workers. They paid 2d a week their employer 1d and the state 1d per week. The insured were to receive 7s 6d per week for five weeks. The principle which Churchill often called 'the magic of numbers, 'bought the miracle of averages to the rescue of the masses.' What was true of commercial insurance did not apply to schemes operated by politicians and bureaucrats. The magic or miracle of commerce could not be reproduced by the state. These contributions were swollen by health insurance and the net arithmetical result was that the employee lost 4d a week deducted from his wages and he was credited with 9d a week. Not surprisingly Lloyd George claimed all the credit for the magic of 4d for 9d when he introduced the combined schemes. The magic held until the First World War, at the outbreak of which there was a credit balance on the scheme of £3 million. But after the war unemployment rose above one million, the account became heavily overdrawn and an expense of the state.

After his death Churchill delivered a eulogy of his old master, Lloyd George 'was the champion of the weak and the poor. Those were great days. Nearly two generations have passed. Most people are unconscious of how much their lives have been shaped by the laws for which Lloyd George was responsible. Health Insurance and Old Age Pensions were the first large-scale State-conscious efforts to set a balustrade along the crowded causeway of the people's life, and without pulling down the structures of society to fasten a lid over the abyss into which vast numbers used to fall, generation after generation, uncared-for and indeed unnoticed.'[1]

The idea that Churchill pioneered the welfare state in close collaboration with Lloyd George during 1908–9 is true. They pretended to have strode a battlefield, but it was as if, instead of marching towards the fire, they had retreated to the medical tent, to weep over the miseries of man.

---

[1] House of Commons 28 March 1943.

8

The People's Budget

On 29 June 1908 Lloyd George, the Chancellor of the Exchequer, told the House of Commons, 'I have no nest eggs. I have to rob somebody's hen roost next year. I am on the lookout which will be the easiest to get and where I shall be least punished, and where I will get the most eggs, and, not only that, but where they can be most easily spared, which is another important qualification'.[1] He and Churchill intended to introduce social reforms on a larger scale than had ever been imagined. Lloyd George wanted the Budget to be much more than a financial measure; it should be a piece of social engineering. He was to build on Asquith's modest deviation from Victorian financial discipline, but go far beyond his modest plan for pensions.

The nineteenth century orthodoxy still declared that additional taxation would depress the economy. Although the screws could no doubt be tightened to some small degree, an altogether new source of taxation was required. The only idea for a novel tax had been Chamberlain's idea of import duties on trade outside the empire. These might be financially attractive, but, in a wider sense, it would involve encumbering the people with the monopolies, privileges, and taxes of protectionism. It was, in reality, a dishonest subterfuge.

In August 1908 Lloyd George travelled through Austria and Germany. On his return he told the Press that he had been 'tremendously impressed with the finished character and perfection of the whole machine' of their social schemes of insurance.

His Treasury staff, then numbering twenty-six, called him 'the Goat', in recognition of both his sexual appetite and his ability to leap in argument from one precarious position to another. He was reckoned a 'non-financial chancellor'. Harcourt told Austin Chamberlain that: 'The trouble with our Lloyd George is . . . that he uses figures exactly as if they were adjectives.'[2] He detested papers and logical thought. He could absorb only an oral briefing and he could think in a dimension widened infinitely by his disregard of the limits which principle or

---

[1] *Hansard* vol. CXCI, cols 395–56.
[2] B. Murray, *The People's Budget 1909–10* p. 81.

probity might have suggested to a more cautious mind. Furthermore, he could convey his understanding and enthusiasms. His mind was undisciplined but alive. 'He was always looking into the next field', observed Churchill and was more concerned with the minds of others rather than his own.

In June 1908 a Cabinet Committee had considered how a Bill to tax land values might be drawn up. On 14 October 1908 Asquith told the House of Commons that a Bill to effect this would be introduced next year. In November 1908 241 Members petitioned Asquith that the measure to value land in Scotland, which the Lords had rejected in 1907, be included for the whole of Britain in the Budget of 1909. The MPs were a disparate group across the parties and had different demands for the taxation of land value. These were Land Reform Association members, thought to number 280, who wanted to make land more accessible and to divert part of land value into private hands, There were 130 land nationalisers, and the single taxers, who wanted taxation to be raised only from land values, whom Josiah Wedgwood estimated numbered seven. The ideas to tax land values were vague. A few wanted to switch taxes from private property i.e. income tax, customs and excise duties to land value. They, Churchill among them, acknowledged that the unimproved value of land was a publicly created fund. Their demand was for an annual tax, equivalent to the annual rental value of land.

However, the great majority, believed, as did Asquith, that only 'windfall' gains accruing to landowners should be claimed by taxation. A windfall gain might accrue from planning permission or from a redevelopment. Suddenly, for example, the owner of a few mangy cattle, grazing on a weed-infested field, happened to reap a fortune following a favourable planning decision. It was evident that richness had been thrust upon him, without any effort of his own. Evidently a tax should be laid upon him.

Lloyd George circulated three examples of a windfall to his Cabinet colleagues. The first was in Abor Valley, near Caerphilly. A village of 300 people, as it had been ten years before, expanded now to accommodate 8000. The landowner drew mining royalties in respect of the coal mined there and collected rent from each cottage. Second, the Barry Dock Company, operating near Cardiff, required a piece of useless foreshore. The landowner charged a rent of £20,000 and exacted the handling charge for the tonnage unloaded there. Third, a village in the Rhondda Valley had enjoyed a population of under 100. It had now expanded to 13,000 inhabitants and the landowner drew rent of £30,000 per annum as well as coal royalties. These examples were clear cases of communal development, but it was extremely difficult to draft legislation to catch windfalls. Indeed chasing windfalls was merely nibbling at the idea of land value taxation. Yet Lloyd George appeared to be dealing with it in a reasonable manner. When Parliament enacts detailed legislation which fails to rectify the ill directly, it delivers the people into the hands of lawyers, entrepreneurs and experts, each of whom think only of their own interests.

Lloyd George was attracted to the idea of including taxes in his Budget designed to catch windfall gains in land. The taxes were novel, mischievous and complex. Here indeed was a nest from which he could take at will. Asquith had long accepted the need to tax land values. On 14 October 1898 he had said that, 'I am convinced of any proposition in politics as I am of any proposition in politics that the next step in the direction of a better municipal life would be, as reason and justice required, for the benefit of the community, [at] the new and hitherto untried source of revenue – a form of taxation which no one thought to be inequitable, because it imposed burdens on those on whom the benefit would ultimately fall.'[1]

To suppose that Asquith planned a collision with the Lords over the Budget in 1909 is to misjudge his character. He was too cautious even to contemplate such a move. Indeed he did not imagine the Lords would reject a money bill, for the constitutional convention that they would let a money bill through, was too well established; they had last refused one about 250 years before. While Lloyd George had no idea that the Lords might reject a Budget, he certainly assembled a provocative package for them. Indeed Churchill had dismissed the possibility in a letter to Asquith on 26 October. 'I learn that Lansdowne in private utterly scouts the suggestion . . .'[2]

On 21 December Lloyd George had said at Liverpool,

> We cannot consent to accept the present humiliating conditions of legislating by the sufferance of Lord Lansdowne. This nobleman has arrogated a position he has usurped – a sovereignty that no king has claimed since the ominous days of Charles I. Decrees are issued from Lansdowne House that Buckingham Palace would not dream of sending forth. We are not going to stand any longer the usurpation of King Lansdowne and his Royal consort in the Commons.[3]

Churchill spoke in Birmingham on 11 January 1909 more belligerently:

> I should be quite content to see the battle joined as speedily as possible upon the plain simple issue of aristocratic power against representative government, between a reversion to protection and the maintenance of free trade, between a tax on bread and a tax on – well never mind.[4]

It seems that they were acting out a common agreement sketched at a long weekend together at Lloyd-George's house at Criccieth in the previous September.

---

[1] *Financial Reform*, Sept–Oct 1898 p. 178.
[2] Chartwell Papers; 2/36, 45.
[3] *Times*, 22 December 1908.
[4] *Times*, 14 January 1909.

Defeat over the dreadnought issue had provided one blade of the shears – defence of the realm – with which they would detach the Lords from its pretended veto. Land value taxation provided the other. Their Lordships, they judged, could not be seen to oppose expense on defence costs by refusing to pay taxation on their considerable land holdings. Indeed they had the Upper House over a barrel and the public would appreciate that posture.

Many have chosen the view that Lloyd George and Churchill were of the same noble and innocent disposition as the Prime Minister. But Asquith was of a different mould; he has often been referred to as 'the last of the Romans', or classical statesman, in British politics. A biographer of Lloyd George has written, 'Lloyd George said he was determined from the start that he would not aim for hwyl and oratory. He had another aim – to set down a manifesto . . . of new principles of a country's taxation, something which he hopes will be referred to and quoted whatever the fate of the Budget.'[1] But Lloyd George varied his tone according to his audience. He could be grave, although by nature he was a comedian.

To summarise this point. Asquith wanted Lloyd George to introduce a radical Budget to enliven a dull mid-session for the Liberals – no election was due for another four years. Yet in the beginning of 1909 Unionists had gained Asburton, Peckham, Ross-on-Wye, Shoreditch, Newcastle-on-Tyne and Pudsey and the Unionists possessed some grounds for claiming that an immediate election would return them a majority. In particular, he wanted to see the Budget used more to address the social problems. He did not believe, however, that the Budget might be used as a battering ram against the House of Lords.

The Budget proposals were subject to much scrutiny before they passed through the Commons but Lloyd George thought the worst opposition to his proposals was from his fellow ministers in the Cabinet. Only Churchill and Morley had mastered the argument for land taxes. The other ministers were either in favour of the windfall concept or they were varying in the degree of their disapproval with the land taxes.

From mid-March to late April the Budget was considered in fourteen cabinet meetings. There are no minutes of these meetings. But the assorted Cabinet papers include a clear summary in six pages of Land Values in New York by Lawson Purdy, the president of Department of Taxes. There were also memorandums by Lloyd George which were unclear and another by Asquith which was more concerned with leases, covenants and other legal matters than the principle of the taxation of land values. But the Cabinet were dominated by Haldane and Reginald McKenna, the latter of whom was described by Balfour as 'an able accountant' – accurate and narrow-minded – and by Lloyd George as 'a banker in blinkers'. McKenna and Haldane and Burns were his main adversaries. Harcourt, a former

[1] J. Grigg, *The People's Champion* p. 193.

Chancellor, and Runciman, the former Financial Secretary, were also ranged against Lloyd George. Crewe and Grey, both conservative Liberals, were silently against him. Burns likened the Cabinet to 'nineteen rag pickers round a heap of muck.'[1] Asquith had decided land taxes of the windfall variety were fair and just and supported the Chancellor in his endeavours to tax them unflinchingly. Lloyd George told Randolph Churchill, Winston's son, in 1930 that, 'Asquith was a much stronger Prime Minister than most people imagined. If he said he would back you up he would see it though. He told me he would support the land taxes. When it came to the final discussion in Cabinet, Asquith asked me to explain the position to them. 'Then he went round every Member for his views. "It seems to me that the weight of the argument rests with the Chancellor." '[2]

The die-hard opponents of the Budget proposals were determined to weaken the land tax proposals; to defeat the proposal of a tax of 1d in the £ on the capital value of land (urban and rural) worth over £50; and to substitute complex and less offensive taxes [in the place of 1d in the £]. This tax was the only effective taxation of land value, but the least popular. In a society which clung tenaciously to the private ownership of land value, this was to be expected. It was a measure which was not supported by the Prime Minister or with any conviction by the Chancellor. 'Mr Lloyd George did not fully understand the implication [of the taxation of land value]. Above all he wanted revenue. Reginald Mckenna did understand too well and defeated the [1d in the £] tax.'[3]

The opposition to the land duties in Cabinet destroyed Lloyd-George's endeavour to tax land values with a direct tax. He could pretend to do so but he had been defeated by Ministers who had a clearer understanding of his measures than he had at that stage. Another means of attack employed by the opponents of the land taxes in Cabinet was a legalistic argument about interfering with existing contracts – tenancies and building agreements principally – in relation to land. In addition, a number of Liberal MPs had advised the Prime Minister that taxing agricultural land was quite unacceptable to them. On 19 March 1909 Asquith's minutes disclose that the Chancellor was defeated over a proposal to tax ground rents of land which had been built upon, because existing contracts would be changed. That was a major defeat. On 24 March the land taxation clauses were 'carefully revised', in an unspecified way, to avoid 'minimising hardship and safeguarding existing contracts.'[4] Lloyd-George's proposals to tax land value were defeated before they were set in print. In the place of a straight tax on land value, the Chancellor cobbled together three taxes on land.

On 3 March Lloyd George checked with Courtney Ibert, the Clerk to the Commons, whether the measures to tax land values could be included in the

---

[1] G. Dangerfield, *The Strange Death of Liberal England* p. 32.
[2] WSC, *Randolph Churchill* vol. 11 pp. 323–24.
[3] J Wedgwood, *Memoirs of a Fighting Life* p. 69.
[4] R. Jenkins, *Asquith* p. 195.

Budget which could contain only measures to raise revenue in the coming year. As they were predicted to become operative in 1909/10 they were allowed to be included in the Budget.

The main problem for Lloyd George was meeting a predicted deficit for 1909/10 of £16.5 million. It was caused principally by the introduction of pensions in the first quarter of 1909. Pensions accounted for £8.7 million. The main expenditure on the dreadnoughts would have to be borne in succeeding financial years. In the current year it was predicted to amount to £2.4 million. Lloyd George raided the Sinking Fund by £3 million, later by a more considerable grab of £3.5 million, but he raised £6.1 million from liquor, tobacco duties, licences and motor duties. The balance was predicted to come from income tax, super taxes, stamp duties and estate duties. The new land taxes were projected to raise £50,0000 in the current year. Lloyd George adjusted the graduation of income tax, which he described as 'the sheet anchor of our financial system'. The purpose of this graduation was to persuade a nation of taxpayers that the richer pay for the poorer.

The liquor duties were revised downwards. The cabinet wanted to fix a maximum charge to a brewer of £500 but agreed eventually to accept Lloyd-George's scale of charges which had the effect of imposing annual charges of about £25,000 on, for example, Guinness and Co. Stamp duties on bills of exchange were scrapped and incomes below £5,000 were protected from the super tax.

The Chancellor spent the Easter recess in Brighton with his Budget team. They found that the estimates were still short of another £500,000. The Budget speech was typed finally by 2 a.m. on the morning of the delivery. Lloyd George walked wearily from the Treasury to the House of Commons on 29 April with Churchill. The previous day Churchill had written to Clementine and described the awaited event as the 'day of wrath'.

The written script of his speech was good enough, but Lloyd George was too exhausted to draw upon his oratory. He spoke for four and a half hours. Balfour kindly suggested the need for the House to adjourn for half an hour to allow the Chancellor a rest. Lloyd-George's daughter Megan remembered Balfour gave him some drink with beef in it. Austin Chamberlain was not none too complimentary when he wrote to his step-mother about the Chancellor' speech:

> Halfway through he was deadbeat, and had to ask for a half hour adjournment. He recovered somewhat after this, but much of his speech was read, and badly read. He stumbled over the sentences, rushed past full stops, paused at the commas and altogether gave the impression that he did not himself understand what he was saying.[1]

---

[1] A. Chamberlain, *Politics from the Inside* p. 177.

This observation was confirmed by Masterman who was sitting with the Chancellor. 'He read from a closely typed manuscript of enormous length. Although a brilliant speaker, he was never a good reader in the House of Commons.'[1] Hilaire Belloc was less indulgent. The budget 'was read', he felt, 'from beginning to end from typewritten notes and was simply deplorable. It lasted four hours of which two and a half consisted of long stupid paragraphs about the rich being rich and the poor being poor.'[2]

Lloyd George added a paragraph to summarise what came to be called 'The People's Budget', to raise the chamber from details to his grand design:

> This is a War Budget. It is for raising money to wage implacable warfare against poverty and squalidness. I cannot help hoping and believing that before this generation has passed away we shall have advanced a great step towards that good time when poverty and wretchedness and human degradation which always follow in its camp will be as remote to the people of this country as the wolves which once infested its forests.[3]

As he made no attempt to remove the cause of poverty, his words seem now to be hollow.

Lloyd George explained the three underlying principles of his Budget. First, the new taxes should be expansive so that they could grow with the increasing expenditure of the State. Second, the taxes should not injure trade and commerce, for they were the springs of national prosperity. Third, all classes had to contribute a fair share of the burdens of taxation.

Normally Lloyd George memorised a speech. But Budget speeches are weighed down by so many boring details, which have increased a thousandfold since 1909. The hope of Asquith's Government that the Budget would be the vanguard of the Liberal economic and social reforms was dashed.

'An amazed Commons found that, instead of provision for the large deficit caused by Old Age Pensions and by Naval Expansion, he was proposing fresh avenues of expenditure and fresh sources of revenue to extend to many years to come.'[4] Leverton Harris, a Unionist Member, told Haldane that the Chancellor appeared not to understand what he was reading. 'Of course he does not', replied Haldane. 'We have been trying for weeks to make him understand clauses of the Bill, and he can't!'[5]

In the historical context a Budget specialist wrote that the Budget 'not only ranged over the whole field of taxation, but was significant for its abandonment

---

[1] L. Masterman, *C.F.G. Masterman* p. 132.
[2] R. Speight, *Hilaire Belloc* p. 223.
[3] *Hansard*, 29 Apri l909 col 546.
[4] L Masterman, *CFG Masterman*, p. 132.
[5] B. Murray, *The People's Budget 1909–10* p. 172.

of the older limitations attaching to the raising of revenue and the open and unqualified adoption of the theory that taxation should be used for the purpose of social regeneration'.[1]

Income tax was raised 2d to 1s 2d in the £, but that pill was sweetened by introducing child allowances and a lower charge on earned than on unearned income. He imposed a graduated supertax of 6d in the £ on those with incomes of more than £5000 and increased death duties by a third to make the rate for estates worth £1 million 15 per cent. A road fund was to be established from duties on vehicles and petrol. He increased duties on tobacco and whisky. Stamp duties were increased.

Churchill warned him not to earn the reputation of a spendthrift Chancellor, but Lloyd George enlarged on plans to establish a Development Fund and to aid aforestation, agriculture, and roads. Then he came to his land taxes. Having rambled through a rather muddled prologue, he leant over backwards not to excite the wrath of landowners and adumbrated the outline of three land taxes. These particular provisions may have been novel to Parliament but many countries, including several colonies, had enacted similar provisions to collect land value.

First, the Increment Value Duty. He imposed this tax of 20 per cent of the growth in value of land after 3 April 1909 when it was sold or transmitted on death. Second, Undeveloped Land Duty was laid at 1s 2d in the £ on land with no improvement made upon it. This was designed to tax land ripe for development while it was being allowed to 'ripen'. Agricultural land (more strictly land under £30 an acre), parks and public spaces were exempt. Third, was the Mineral Rights Duty which had nothing to do with land value; it was 1d in the £ assessed on mineral right rentals. Fourth, the Reversion Duty did not apply to land value either; it was levied on building land at the rate of 10 per cent upon the expiration of leases.

The Increment Value Duty was proposed by McKenna.[2] It was a proportion of the land value which could easily be expressed as a small part of the total value of a hereditament. It was assessable on the capital increment occurring after the Budget and was assessed only on death or sale, rather than annually. The Undeveloped Land Duty was set at a ridiculously low level. There was so many allowable deductions that it was both hard to collect and difficult to understand.

Neither the Mineral Rights Duty nor the Reversion Duty were taxes on land value.

This brief summary is, however, greatly simplified. For it ignores the calculations of the assessable value. First, there was a 'gross value' of land – market value of the unencumbered fee simple; then the 'full site value'-gross value less

---

[1] B. Mallet, *British Budgets 1880–1913*; pp. 298–99.
[2] Lord Wedgwood, *Testament to Democracy*, p. 130.

the value of buildings and improvements on the land ; then the 'total value' of land-gross value less any public charge and finally, 'assessable site value'-total value after deduction of value of buildings from the gross value. The valuation and incidence of the taxes would be a lawyers' picnic.

The complexity of the four duties and the four values was evidence of muddled thinking. Lloyd George had attempted to pull off a popular reform. Having done something similar, he was able to pretend that he had done so. But when one examines his measures there is no doubt that he had failed; indeed he had failed utterly to return the value to the community, which had created it. His original attempt to tax land value had been thwarted by his Cabinet colleagues, who forced him to introduce three useless measures.

The only virtue that could be claimed initially for his measures was that he had created the mechanism for the valuation of land. But he extended this valuation to include the valuation of buildings, woodlands and farm machinery. The valuation process proved costly, tedious and wearisome.

The grand concept which lay behind the taxation of land values, the division of property into public and private, had been evoked, betrayed and laid waste. It had been destroyed by determined opposition in Cabinet. Lloyd George did not understand the implications of what his colleagues had done.

9

Rejection by the House of Landlords

Balfour uttered his criticism of the Budget in the Commons on 3 May 1909.

'So blind and ignorant are you, [he hissed at the Chancellor], of the fact that it is impossible to attack one kind of property, arbitrarily selected, without throwing a shade of fear on security and suspicion over every other class of property. Much of the evil you have done has been done even by the fact of your proposals. Whatever the House may do with them, I am quite sure has disturbed the mind of everyone who reflects upon the many occasions which an individualistic society – so long as it lasts – can flourish. Your scheme is arbitrary and unjust.'[1]

His spluttering rage was not backed by any semblance of reasoning.

Balfour had dismissed earlier the idea that the unearned increment bestowed on landowners by the opening of a railway line was created by society. He attributed the creation of land value to small individuals such as market gardeners. He thought no one would tax the railway company or the farmer for this unearned increment, which resulted from the interplay of the development of agriculture and railways. It is a perennial trick of Tories to pretend worthy and insignificant figures were their main concern and in need of their protection. Market gardeners and widows, were old favourites employed to draw attention away from the larger landowners. Writing to his niece two months later Balfour dismissed the Budget by alleging that 'the motive of the Government in putting [the land taxes] on was to please the "mass" of the voters, or, as your friend puts it "the poor". This is precisely the crime that lies at their door. They have chosen a particular section of the community, and a particular kind of property which they think, both unpopular and helpless, and have proceeded to mulct it – demagogism in its worst aspect.'[2]

Though Joe Chamberlain had been disabled by a stroke, he returned

---

[1] Hansard 3 May 1909 col 773.
[2] K. Baker, *Arthur James Balfour* p. 287.

immediately from the South of France to stiffen the fight against the Budget. It represented an attack on his argument that new revenue could be found only from tariffs imposed on trade. The Budget was, indeed, a rival model to that of tariff reform.

Earlier in his career Chamberlain had ridiculed the Lords. He had said on 4 August 1884 during a speech at Bingley Hall, Birmingham: 'The House of Lords for one hundred years has never contributed one iota to popular liberties, or anything to advance the commonweal and during that time it has protected every abuse and sheltered every privilege. It has denied justice and delayed every reform. It is obstinate without courage, arbitrary without judgement, and arrogant without knowledge.' Gladstone had questioned about the intemperance of the language and Chamberlain considered the speech and commented: 'I also attacked the pretensions of the House of Lords and said that the divine right of Kings was a dangerous delusion but the divine right of peers would be a ridiculous absurdity'.[1] But after the Budget Chamberlain saw the House of Lords as the last refuge of sanity. While the Unionists leaders were advising caution in handling the Budget, Chamberlain demanded its outright rejection by their Lordships.

The passage of the Budget and the Finance Bill involved the House of Commons for seventy days and caused 554 divisions – then said to be the longest in living memory. The House was in continuous session from the end of April until November 1909. It was not that the the Finance Bill was scrutinised section by section, but, according to the Chancellor, it was attacked 'on practically two proposals, land and licences'.[2] Asquith observed that the attacks on the Budget were 'mainly, if not exclusively, confined to these taxes.'[3] The main opposition attack was mounted by a Member who might have been the landlord's paw: E. Pretyman. He described the land clauses as 'unfair', 'ludicrous', 'unjust', 'monstrous', 'preposterous' and 'impossible'. The Labour members welcomed the Budget, apart from tax on tobacco, but the Irish Nationalists did not; they believed in Protection and they hated tax on whiskey. The Unionists let the ordinary financial measures – the increases in income tax, estate duty and the like – through with customary reluctance. They reserved their opposition for the land value tax clauses. So many were their amendments that the Prime Minister introduced the 'kangaroo' by which the Chairman was allowed, with the leave of the House, to accept amendments. Balfour was not agreeable to this device; he attacked it as 'martial law'.

A Finance Bill, containing the small print of the Budget, was not the sort of adventure Churchill relished. It was so tedious in its details, its compromises and its debates. 'His [Churchill's] great weakness, which is growing on him more and more, is his love of limelight; of always wanting to be in the public eye; and the

---

[1] J. Chamberlain, *A Political Memoir 1880–92* p. 97–8.
[2] *The Peoples' Budget*, Foreword by Lloyd-George p. 61.
[3] Liberal Publications, *The Land Value Taxes* A Speech by Asquith p. 7.

assiduity in learning, which he certainly had when he was younger, he was beginning to lose.'[1] The proceedings might be riveting to various interests and their professional advisers, who hoped for a loophole or concession. Churchill managed, however, to speak briefly in the debate in early May and again in June. ' "You see", he said one evening to [Lloyd George], "in spite of your trying to keep me out of the Budget, I made a show after all." "I like that", said Lloyd George, I offered to hand you then whole of Part 11, the income tax. "Oh, that's detail!" said Winston scornfully, "I am not going to do detail . . ." '[2] In fact the Budget had become bogged down in its detail and its underlying principles quite forgotten.

In mid-May leading figures in the City wrote a letter of protest to Asquith. They did not like the Budget. They denounced it as socialist and subversive. The City has ever been the citadel of conservatism. They had never liked change. They had defeated reform on several occasions; particularly when it has effected the taxation of land value; not by argument but furtively by, for example, causing a financial crisis.

During the summer months of 1909, nothing much apart from the Budget was debated by the Commons. Churchill did manage to introduce two Bills setting up Labour Exchanges and Trade Boards.

Lloyd George distinguished himself in handling much of the details of Finance Bill. 'On the whole', observed Masterman, 'the Opposition are very fond of George. He amuses Arthur Balfour by his quickness and acuteness, and he has a kind of magnetism over the whole House possessed by very few others.'[3] Lloyd George voted in 462 divisions. He was relieved by Haldane, Asquith, Churchill and others. Once it was objected that Churchill was present in his pyjamas – he wore them under his suit. Although Churchill's voting record was the worst of the Cabinet, he was active outside Parliament. There was a certain rivalry between Lloyd George and him. Churchill remained throughout on friendly terms with Lloyd George – one of the few to call him David.

'Lloyd George and Churchill were on the bench together just after the birth of Winston's daughter (Diana on 4 May 1909). "Is she a pretty child?" asked Lloyd George. "The prettiest child I have ever seen", said Winston beaming. "Like her mother, I suppose?" said George. "No", said Winston, still more gravely, "she is exactly like me." '[4]

During the year of 1909 relations between Churchill and Lloyd George matured. On 3 November Churchill touched on this subject in a letter to his wife. 'I am in quite friendly relations with LG but more formal and independent than before.'

On 24 June Lloyd George spoke at Holborn which is about as close to the City

---

[1] L Masterman, *C.F.G Masterman*, p. 154.
[2] Ibid pp. 154–5.
[3] Ibid p. 142.
[4] Ibid p. 144.

as argument can be tolerated. 'We had simply', he bantered, 'the same old drivel about socialism and, of course, the thin end of the wedge – it is becoming very thin indeed by constant use ... Then of course there was the inevitable Lord Rothschild. He said that the Budget was Socialism and Collectivism. Now I wonder whether he knows what socialism means. I am sure he does not. I suppose it would be too much to ask a financier ruined by the Budget to spend any money on political literature; but I think it would be money very well spent ... if someone would present him with a sixpenny handbook on Socialism ...'

A month later a leading Unionist, Walter Lang, formed a Budget Protest League to fight the Finance Bill outside Parliament. The Prime Minister thought that a movement should be started to promote the Budget's principles. Accordingly, the Liberal Party responded by forming the Budget League, and Churchill, their main platform asset, was elected its President.

Churchill loved the opportunity to contribute his oratory and enthusiasm to the budget campaign. He addressed meetings throughout the country. They meetings were begun and concluded with singing *The Land Song* to the tune of *Marching through Georgia*. The words were:

> *The land, the land,*
> *The ground on which we stand,*
> *T'was God who gave the land to the people,*
> *Why should we be beggars with the ballot in our hand,*
> *When God gave the land to the people.*
>
> *We are going into battle.*
> *Let us stand together like comrades and brothers.*
> *The issues are very simple, but they are very great.*
> *We have to drive the Budget through.*
> *We have to smash the veto up, and if we march together*
> *There is none that can withstand us.*

Churchill was drawing abuse and enjoying himself by being provocative over the grand scheme of the Budget, rather than its uninspiring details. In Norwich on 26 July he referred to the passage of the Finance Bill.

Across and beyond the complicated details of the order paper, the absurd obstruction, the dry discussion in Committee, the interminable repetition of divisions, the angry scenes which flash up from time to time, the white-faced members sitting the whole night through and walking home worn out in the full light of morning – across and beyond all this, can you not discern a people's cause in conflict? Can you not see a great effort to make a big step forward towards that brighter and more equal world for which, be sure, those who after us will hold our names in honour?[1]

   This type of political activity lured Lloyd George to slip away from his sacerdotal duties at Westminster. At Limehouse, in east London, on 30 July he spoke to an audience of about 4000. That was much more enjoyable for the Chancellor than speaking to to Mr Pretyman in an otherwise deserted Commons He declared:

> When the Prime Minister and I knock at the door of these great landlords and say to them – "Here, you know these poor fellows have been digging up royalties at the risk of their lives, some of them are old, they have survived the perils of their trade, they are broken, they can earn no more. Won't you give them something to keep them out of the workhouse?" They scowl at you and we say "Only a ha'penny, just a copper". They say, "You thieves!" And they turn their dogs onto us, and every day you can hear their bark. [Loud laughter and cheers] We started building [dreadnoughts]; we wanted money to pay for the building; so we sent the hat round. We sent it around among workmen they all dropped in their coppers. We went round Belgravia and there has been such a howl ever since that it has well-nigh deafened us. It is rather a shame that a rich country like ours should allow those who have toiled all their days to end in penury and possibly starvation. It is rather hard that an old workman should have to find his way to the gates of the tomb, bleeding and footsore, through the brambles and thorns of poverty. We cut a new path for him – an easier one, a pleasanter one, through fields of waving corn ... There are many in this country blessed by Providence with great wealth, and if there are amongst them men who grudge out of their riches a fair contribution towards the less fortunate of their fellow countrymen they are very shabby rich men. The landowner did not earn his wealth: his sole function, his chief pride, is stately consumption of wealth produced by others.[2]

   The speech was resented by the established orthodoxy. F. E. Smith called it the 'Slimehouse speech'. The King, Edward VII, unsurprisingly, was annoyed by the Chancellor. He complained to the Prime Minister at Cowes. For the hereditary peerage was a main buttress of the royal claim to a hereditary throne. Edward also protested through his secretary, Lord Knollys, to his close friend Lord Crewe, the Colonial Secretary: 'that the speech was full of falsity and of Socialism in its most insidious form and of virulent abuse against one particular class', could 'only have

---

[1] *Times* 27 July 1909.
[2] *Times*, 31 July 1909.

the effect of stirring up "class" against "class", and of stirring up the worst possible passions of its audience. It is hardly necessary, perhaps, to allude to its gross vulgarity.'[1] The language employed at Limehouse was that of Billingsgate. The Chancellor had even transgressed the limits of taste which the established order applied to Welsh Nonconformists. Lloyd George wrote to the king to say that he had been provoked and the king replied to stress the difference between a backbench Member, who could say what he liked, and a leading member of the cabinet, who had to observe the traditions of his office. In fact, the king liked Lloyd George and had declined to offer any advice on the Budget of 1909.

The speech at Limehouse caused a stir in Liberal ranks. For when it came to taxation of land value, many party members were as much dominated by their vested interest as the Unionists. Viscount Esher gained the impression over a lunch with Balfour in November that: 'Certainly from the day of Lloyd George's speech at Limehouse the fate of the budget was sealed.'[2]

Limehouse marked a change of attitude in Lloyd George towards a possible rejection by the Lords. He told the Masterman, 'I am not sure we ought to pray for it to go through. I am not sure we ought not to hope for its rejection. It would give us a chance as we shall never see again.'[3]

On 4 September Churchill started out more gravely in a speech at Leicester:

> We are at a crossroads. If we stand in a happy-go-lucky way, the richer classes ever growing in wealth and in number, and ever declining in responsibility, the very poor remaining plunged or plunging deeper into helpless, hopeless misery, then I think there is nothing before us but savage strife between class and class, with ever increasing disorganisation, with an increasing destruction of human strength and virtue – nothing, in fact, but that dual degeneration, which comes from the simultaneous waste of extreme wealth and extreme want, the unnatural gap between rich and poor, the divorce of the people from the land, the want of proper discipline and training in our youth, the exploitation of boy labour, the physical degeneration which seems to follow so swiftly on civilised poverty, the awful jumbles of an obsolete Poor Law, the horrid havoc of the liquor traffic, the constant insecurity in the means of subsistence and employment which breaks the heart of many a sober, hard-working man, the absence of any established minimum standard of life and comfort among the workers, and, at the other end, the swift increase of vulgar, joyless luxury – here are the enemies of Britain . . . the tax-gatherer would now ask not what you have got, but how did you get it?

[1] R. Churchill, *Winston S. Churchill* vol ii p. 326.
[2] K. Young, *Arthur James Balfour* p. 290.
[3] L. Masterman, *C.F.G. Masterman* pp. 140–3.

Churchill included some ridicule of the opponents of the Budget. He referred to:

> the small fry of the Tory party splashing actively in their proper puddles. (Balfour) – who aims to lead – who has been meaning to lead for six years if only he could find out where on earth to lead to. They (the Tories) have been forced to fall back on their dukes. These unfortunate individuals who ought to lead quiet, delicate, sheltered lives, far from the madding crowd's ignoble strife, have been dragged into the football scrimmage, and they have got rather roughly mauled in the process . . . Do not let us be too hard on them. It is a poor sport – almost like teasing goldfish . . . These ornamental creatures caught on every hook they seek, and there is no sport whatever in catching them. It would be barbarous to leave them gasping on the bank of public ridicule upon which they have landed themselves. Let us put them back gently, tenderly into their fountains – and if a few bright scales have been rubbed off in what the Prime Minister calls the variegated handling they have received, they will soon get over it . . . If the struggle comes, it will be between a representative assembly and a miserable minority of titled persons who represent nobody, who are responsible to nobody, who only scurry up to London to vote in their party interests, their class interests and in their own interests.[1]

In his speech Churchill had attacked a less ornamental creature: 'It is quite true', he said, 'that Mr Balfour from time to time emits four or five columns of insipid equivocation which the newspaper whose proprietors he has taken the precaution of making into barons, hasten to claim another epoch-making pronouncement'.

Lord Knollys wrote to *The Times* on 11 September in order to deliver a petty and terse rebuke. 'I beg to inform you that notwithstanding Winston Churchill's statement, the creation of peers remains a royal prerogative'. Churchill commented next day in a letter to Clementine 'He and the King have really gone mad . . . This looks to me like a remarkable Royal intervention and shows the bitterness which is felt in those circles. I shall take no notice of it. It will defeat itself.'[2]

Lloyd George could not be restrained and at Newcastle on 9 October before 5200 at the Palace Theatre he slipped the royal leash which had been thrown around him after his speech at Limehouse.

> Only one stock has gone down badly – there has been a great slump in dukes. They used to stand rather high in the market, especially the Tory

---

[1] *Times* 6 September 1909.
[2] R. Churchill, *Winston S. Churchill* vol ii p. 327.

market, but the Tory Press has just discovered that they are of no value. ... A fully-equipped duke costs twice as much to keep up as two dreadnoughts – and they are just as great a terror – and they last longer. As long as they were content to be mere idols on their pedestals, preserving that stately science which became their rank and their intelligence, all went well and the average British citizen looked up to them ... But then came the Budget. They stepped off their perch. They have been scolding like omnibus drivers purely because the Budget cart has knocked a little of the gilt off their old stage coach ... Who made ten thousand people owners of the soil, and the rest of us trespassers in the land of our birth? Who is it who is responsible for the scheme of things whereby one man is engaged through life in grinding labour to win a bare and precarious living for himself, and when, at the end of his days, he claims at the hand of the community he served a poor pension of eighteen pence a day, and another man who does not toil receives every hour of the day and every hour of the night, whilst he slumbers, more than his poor neighbour receives in a whole year of toil?' He left his audience with a simple question to ponder: 'Should five hundred men [the peers], ordinary men chosen accidentally among the unemployed, override the judgment – the deliberate judgement – of millions of people who are engaged in the industry which makes the wealth of the country?'[1]

Lloyd George savoured the delight in the summer of 1909 in ridiculing landlords and their apologists. 'The land in London is worth more than all the municipal debt in the kingdom. Who created that wealth? It was not the landlords. London was a swamp and the landlords did not even create that' or, 'the rich man can afford to be ignorant; the poor man cannot' or, 'the idle rich – my opponents emphasise the word rich; it is the adjective which I put in italics.'[2]

Until late in the summer attention had centered on the House of Commons, but gradually the peerage came clumsily onto the public stage. Their Lordships were not disturbed about the extra expense of dreadnoughts. Defence of the realm was not an issue on which they would ever consider making a fuss. It was the land taxes which stuck in their noble throat. To talk of land taxation to the Lords, remarked Lord Morley [as he became]), was like talking to a butcher about Lent.

On 16 July Lord Lansdowne, the Tory leader, stated that the House of Lords 'would not swallow the Finance Bill without wincing' and when that was mis-reported as 'mincing' Churchill could not resist speculating. In Edinburgh he offered his Lordships advice, either mince the Budget and eat their own mince or

---

[1] *Times*, 11 Oct. 1909.
[2] D. Rider, *Wit and Wisdom of Lloyd-George* pp. 44–5.

risk chastisement from the election. At that time no definite decision had been taken on the action of the Unionist peers. A few rural potentates warned in preparation for an attack on the Bill. In June Lord Onslow and Lord Sherbone uttered grave warnings about selling part of their estates and neglecting their upkeep. On 7 August the Duke of Beaufort, who owned 51,085 acres, inveighed menacingly at a puppy walking in Cirencester 'I would love to see Winston Churchill and Lloyd George in the middle of twenty couples of dog hounds'. The Duke of Buccleugh, who owned 400,000 acres, refused to donate an annual subscription to Dumfries Football Club, 'owing', he excused himself,' to the large prospective increase in taxation caused by the present Budget'. His economy was made good by a number of Liberal members of parliament. The Duke of Rutland described them as 'tatterdalmatians.' The Earl of Haddington sent a subscription of £5 to the Cheshire Agricultural Society but with a thrifty note that, 'owing to recent legislation I find that I must reduce the amount of my principal usual subscriptions to the CAS to three guineas in future'. The Duke of Portland, who owned 183,199 acres, explained on 31 August at Welbeck that, 'About £1,000 a week was spent on his estate in wages, and nearly a thousand individuals were employed. It was too obvious that, through no ill will of his, this sum would have to be largely diminished in the new circumstances created by the Budget.' The Earl of Derby declined a similar subscription more succinctly, with the words 'under present circumstances'.[1] These noble reactions exasperated Joynson-Hicks, a Conservative Member. He only wished that before Budget Day that 'every Duke had been locked up and kept locked up until this Budget was over . . . These men who are going about squealing and say that they are going to reduce their subscriptions to charities and football clubs . . . ought to be ashamed of themselves.'[2]

Churchill kept a note which listed the landholdings of the twenty-three dukes. In sum they owned 3.5 million acres. But the argument was not about possession of land but rather about possession of its value. This list showed how the dukes had accumulated vast private property and it was information that be could used in many an encounter. It could be contrasted, for example, with the chilling fact that twenty-three million adults owned not a square inch of their planet; indeed they were landless trespassers.

Lord Rosebery, a former Liberal Prime Minister, objected with the same instinctive and unthinking knee-jerk of the Lords. He denounced the Budget as 'the end of all, the negation of faith, of family, of property, of Monarchy, of Empire'. The Opposition seized on his denunciation. As the Finance Bill moved towards the Upper House, Lord Lansdowne received the reactions of his more thoughtful and literary fellows. Indeed they shared the gut feeling of less urbane

---

[1] V. Bonham Carter, *Churchill As I Knew Him* p. 182.
[2] E. Allyn, *Lords versus Commons* p. 180.

peers. On 11 September Lord Rosebery denounced it in a speech at Glasgow: it was 'a revolution without popular mandate.'[1] By mid-September 1909, by which time it was clear the Finance Bill had survived the Opposition's fury in the Commons, Balfour was promoting his threat that: 'if the Lords do not reject the Bill, he could not continue to lead the party'.[2] It was his final attempt to defeat the Finance Bill. He had failed to have it amended, delayed or defeated in the country or the Commons.

Lord Lytton wrote to Lansdowne on 8 October to propose a reasonable course, based on insight into the bungled Budget, rather than Unionist instinct, and its failings. He saw that if left to run its course the budget would fall apart. 'If . . . the Budget were allowed to pass, its burdens would soon prove odious in practice, and the comforting theory on which it is now founded would be exploded. By the end of the year the Government would have to go to the country and, I believe, suffer defeat.' But to merely talk of taxing land value was to Lansdowne like unfurling a revolution. He had set his course resolutely on rejection, though a few days earlier he and Balfour had assured the King that their minds were not yet decided on the treatment of the Budget. He explained it in a letter to Lord Burleigh on 21 October that he was attracted by the idea of amendment. It was an idea which had aroused interest 'amongst rather crotchety folk'. However, 'if the Lords amended the licensing and land provisions the House of Lords would risk being accused of deserting their fellow-sufferers and thinking of their own skins'. In any case amendment would raise the technical debate about money bills and the tacking on of other measures. It was, therefore, a question of either accepting or rejecting the whole. 'I am in favour', Lord Lansdowne stated, 'of rejection, upon the broad ground that the Finance Bill is a new departure of the most dangerous kind, to which the House of Lords has no right to assent until it is sure that Her Majesty's Government have the support of the country . . . I do not believe the country desires a single-chamber system.'

On 10 November Lansdowne gave public notice of his intention to reject and during the debate on second reading Lord Reay, a Liberal peer, warned the Lords not to 'forget the lessons of history, that oligarchies are seldom destroyed and more frequently commit suicide.'[3] The Lords approved Landsdowne's motion on the second reading 'That this House is not justified in giving its consent to this Bill until it has been submitted to the judgment of the country.'[4] It was a clever motion. After five days of debate they voted by 350–75 to accept the motion, thereby rejecting the Budget of 1909.

In a later speech at Plymouth, Lansdowne referred to features of the Budget which had particularly struck his House. It created a colossal deficit, the

[1] B Murray, *The People's Budget 1909–10* p. 231.
[2] A. Chamberlain, *Politics From The Inside* p. 182.
[3] Official Reports Lords 1909, vol 1V 1193.
[4] Lord Newton, *Lord Lansdowne* p. 80.

Chancellor 'had raided the Sinking Fund', it had 'created panic destructive of confidence and credit, in consequence unemployment has come into our midst.'[1]

Two constitutional lawyers of the highest repute, Professor Dicey and Sir William Anson, thought the rejection was reasonable. Lest it be thought that these were the disinterested opinions of two eminent academic jurists, it should be added that they were Unionists who supported the Lords ardently. Years later Sir Austen Chamberlain reflected that, 'it must be admitted that it was a mistake for the House of Lords to throw out the Budget at first instance.'[2]

Following the rejection by the House of Lords, the Prime Minister tabled a Cabinet resolution: 'that the action of the House of Lords in refusing to pass into law the financial provision made by the House for the Service of the year is a breach of the Constitution and an usurpation of the Commons.' On 2 December 1909 he moved the resolution. He dismissed the idea that the Commons would produce a new Bill

> pruned and trimmed and refurbished to accommodate the wishes of their Lordships operating new-fangled Caesarism which converts the House of Lords into a kind of plebiscitary organ ... They have elected to set at nought in regard to finance the unwritten but time-honoured conventions of our Constitution. In doing so, whether they foresaw it or not, they have opened out a wider and more far-reaching issue. We have not provoked the challenge, but we welcome it. We believe that the first principles of representative government ... are at stake, and we ask the House of Commons ... as ... we shall ask the constituencies of this country, to declare that the organ, the voice of the free people of this country is to be found in the elected representatives of the nation.

Battle lines had been drawn between the two Houses of Parliament and next day the Prime Minister called a General Election. 'The Lords may decree a revolution,' Lloyd George had earlier predicted, 'but the people will direct it.'[3]

---

[1] WSC, *The People's Rights* 1970 edn. p. 34.
[2] A. Chamberlain, *Politics From The Inside*; p. 320.
[3] P. Rowland, *Lloyd George* p. 222.

10

Churchill's speech in Edinburgh

The Budget League, formed by the Liberal Government, was directed by Churchill to promote the Budget, and operated from July to November 1909. It arranged forty meetings for Cabinet ministers, 731 for Members of Parliament and 3564 other meetings. It distributed 17 million leaflets and 680,000 posters.

Churchill delivered some memorable speeches in that summer. He loved the public platform, a grand political idea and the large public meeting. How he loathed attendance at Westminster when they debated the detail of some Finance Bill. For the debate was dry, the speakers were dull and the Bill before and after amendment was unreadable.

The speech he delivered at the King's Theatre in Edinburgh especially stands out. It represents the apogee of the Liberal government's attempt to recover for the community the value of land which it had created. It ranks as a fine exposition of the land value case.

As reported in *The Times*, Churchill's speech on 17 July 1909 at the King's Theatre speaks for itself. His powerful comprehension was the foundation of his speech and his brilliant command of language formed its structure.

> We are often assured by sagacious persons that the civilisation of modern states is largely based upon respect for the rights of private property. If that be true, it is also true that such respect cannot be secured, and ought not, indeed, to be expected, unless property is associated in the minds of the great mass of the people with the ideas of justice and of reason.
>
> It is, therefore, of the first importance to the country – to any country – that there should be vigilant and persistent efforts to prevent abuses, to distribute the public burdens fairly among all classes, and to establish good laws governing the methods by which wealth may be acquired. The best way to make private property secure and respected is to bring the processes by which it is gained into harmony with the general interests of the public. When and where property is associated with the idea of reward for services rendered, with the idea of recompense for high gifts and special aptitudes or for faithful labour done, then property will be

101

honoured. When it is associated with processes which are beneficial, or which at the worse are not actually injurious to the common wealth, then property will be unmolested; but when it is associated with ideas of wrong and of unfairness, with processes of restriction and monopoly, and other forms of injury to the community, then I think that you will find that property will be assailed and will be endangered.

A year ago I was fighting an election in Dundee. In the course of that election I attempted to draw a fundamental distinction between the principles of Liberalism and of Socialism, and I said 'Socialism attacks capital; Liberalism attacks monopoly.' And it is from that fundamental distinction that I come directly to the land proposals of the present Budget.

It is quite true that the land monopoly is not the only monopoly which exists, but it is by far the greatest of monopolies; it is a perpetual monopoly, and it is the mother of all other forms of monopoly. It is quite true that unearned increments in land are not the only form of unearned or undeserved profit which individuals are able to secure; but it is the principal form of unearned increment, derived from processes, which are merely not beneficial, but which are positively detrimental to the general public. Land, which is a necessity of human existence, which is the original source of all wealth, which is strictly limited in extent, which is fixed in geographical position – land, I say, differs from all other forms of property in this primary and fundamental conditions.

Nothing is more amusing than to watch the efforts of our monopolist opponents to prove that other forms of property and increment are exactly the same and are similar in all respects to the unearned increment in land. They talk to us of the increased profits of a doctor or a lawyer from the growth of population in the towns in which they live. They talk to us of the profits of a railway through a greater degree of wealth and activity in the districts through which it runs. They tell us of the profits which are derived from a rise in stocks and shares, and even of those which are sometimes derived from the sale of pictures and works of art, and they ask us – as if it were their only complaint – 'Ought not all these other forms to be taxed too?'

But see how misleading and false all these analogies are. The windfalls which people with artistic gifts are able from time to time to derive from the sale of a picture – from a Van Dyck or a Holbein – may here and there be very considerable but pictures do not get in anybody's way. They do not lay a toll on anybody's labour; they do not touch enterprise and production at any point; they do not affect any of those creative processes upon which the material well-being of millions depends. And if a rise in stocks and shares confers profits on the fortunate holders far beyond what they expected, or, indeed, deserved, nevertheless, that profit has not been reaped by with-holding from the community the land which it needs, but, on the contrary, apart from mere gambling, it has been reaped by supplying industry with the capital without which it could not be carried on.

If the railway makes greater profits, it is usually because it carries more goods and more passengers. If a doctor or a lawyer enjoys a better practice, it is because the doctor attends more patients and more exacting patients, and because the lawyer pleads more suits in the courts and more important suits. At every stage the doctor or the lawyer is giving service in return for his fees; and if the service is too poor or the fees are too high, other doctors and other lawyers can come freely into competition. There is constant service, there is constant competition; there is no monopoly, there is no injury to the public interest, there is no impediment to the general progress.

Fancy comparing these healthy processes with the enrichment which comes to the landlord who happens to own a plot of land on the outskirts or at the centre of one of our great cities, who watches the busy population around him making the city larger, richer, more convenient, more famous every day, and all the while sits still and does nothing! Roads are made, streets are made, railway services are improved, electric light turns night into day, electric trams glide swiftly to and fro, water is brought from reservoirs a hundred miles off in the mountains – and all the while the landlord sits still. Every one of those improvements is effected by the labour and at the cost of other people. Many of the most important are effected at the cost of the municipality and of the ratepayers. To not one of those improvements does the land monopolist, as a land monopolist, contribute, and yet by every one of them the value of his land is sensibly enhanced.

He renders no service to the community, he contributes nothing to the general welfare, he contributes nothing even to the process from which his own enrichment is derived. If the land were occupied by shops or by dwellings, the municipality at least would secure the rates upon them in aid of the general fund; but the land may be unoccupied, undeveloped, it may be what is called 'ripening' – ripening at the expense of the whole city, of the whole country – for the unearned increment of its owner. Roads perhaps have to be diverted to avoid this forbidden area. The merchant going to his office, the artisan going to his work, have to make a detour or pay a tram fare to avoid it. The citizens are losing their chance of developing the land, the city is losing its rates, the State is losing its taxes which would have accrued, if the natural development had taken place – and that share has to be replaced at the expense of the other ratepayers and tax-payers; and the nation as a whole is losing in the competition of the world – the hard and growing competition in the world both in time and money. And all the while the land monopolist has only to sit still and watch complacently his property multiplying in value, sometimes manifold, without either effort or contribution on his part. And that is justice!

But let us follow the process a little farther. The population of the city grows and grows still larger year by year, the congestion in the poorer quarters becomes acute, rents and rates rise hand in hand, and thousands of families are crowded into one-roomed tenements. There are 120,000 persons living in one roomed tenements in Glasgow alone at the present time. At last the land becomes ripe for sale – that means that the price is too tempting to be resisted any longer – and then, and not till then it is sold by the yard or by the inch at ten times, or twenty times, or even fifty times, its agricultural value, on which alone hitherto it has been rated for the public service.

The greater the population around the land, the greater the injury which they have sustained by its protracted denial the more inconvenience which has been caused to everybody, the more serious the loss in economic strength and activity, the larger will be the profit of the landlord when the sale is finally accomplished. In fact you may say that the unearned increment on the land is on all-fours with the profit gathered by one of those American speculators who engineer a corner in corn, or meat, or cotton, or some other vital commodity, and that the unearned increment in land is reaped by the land monopolist in exact proportion, not to the service, but to the disservice done.

It is monopoly which is the keynote; and where monopoly prevails, the greater the injury to society, the greater the reward of the monopolist will be. See how this evil process strikes at every form of industrial activity. The municipality, wishing for broader streets, better houses, more healthy, decent, scientifically planned towns, is made to pay, and is made to pay in exact proportion, or to a very great extent in proportion as it has exerted itself in the past to make improvements. The more it has improved the town, the more it has increased the land value, and the more it will have to pay for any land it may wish to acquire. The manufacturer purposing to start a new industry, proposing to erect a great factory offering employment to thousands of hands, is made to pay such a price for his land that the purchase-price hangs round the neck of his whole business, hampering his competitive power in every market, clogging him far more than any foreign tariff in his export competition; and the land values strike down through the profits of the manufacturer on to the wages of the workman. The railway company wishing to build a new line finds that the price of land which yesterday was only rated at its agricultural value has risen to a prohibitive figure the moment it was known that the new line was projected; and either the railway is not built, or, if it is, is built only on terms which largely transfer to the landowner the profits which are due to the shareholders and the advantages which should have accrued to the travelling public.

It does not matter where you look or what examples you select, you will see that every form of enterprise, every step in material progress, is only undertaken after the land monopolist has skimmed the cream off for himself, and everywhere today the man, or the public body, who wishes to put land to its highest use is forced to pay a preliminary fine in land values to the man who is putting it to an inferior use, and in some cases to no use at all. All comes back to the land value, and its owner for the time being is able to levy his toll upon all other forms of wealth and upon every form of industry. A portion, in some cases the whole, of every benefit which is laboriously acquired by the community is represented in the land value, and finds its way automatically into the landlord's pocket. If there is a rise in wages, rents are able to move forward, because the workers can afford to pay a little more. If the opening of a new railway or a new tramway, or the institution of an improved service of workmen's trains, or a lowering of fares, or a new invention, or any other public convenience affords a benefit to the workers in any particular district, it becomes easier for them to live, and therefore the landlord and the ground landlord, one on top of the other, are able to charge them more for the privilege of living there.

Some years ago in London there was a toll-bar on a bridge across the Thames [Waterloo Bridge], and all the working people who lived on the south side of the river, had to pay a daily toll of one penny for going and returning from their work. The spectacle of these poor people thus mulcted of so large a proportion of their earnings appealed to the public conscience: an agitation was set on foot, municipal authorities were roused, and at the cost of the rate payers the bridge was freed [in 1878] and the toll removed. All those people who used the bridge were saved 6d. a week. Within a very short period from that time the rents on the south side of the river were found to have advance by about 6d a week, or the amount of the toll which had been remitted. And a friend of mine was telling me the other day that in the parish of Southwark about £350 a year, roughly speaking, was given away in doles of bread by charitable people in connection with one of the churches, and as a consequence of this the competition for small houses, but more particularly for single-roomed tenements is, we are told, so great that rents are considerably higher than in the neighbouring district.

All goes back to the land, and the landowner, who in many cases, in most cases, is a worthy person utterly unconscious of the character of the methods by which he is enriched, is enabled with resistless strength to absorb to himself a share of almost every public and every private benefit, however important or however pitiful those benefits may be.

I hope you will understand that when I speak of the land monopolist, I am dealing more with the process than with the individual landowner. I have no wish to hold any class up to public disapprobation. I do not think that the man who makes money by unearned increment in land, is morally a worse man than anyone else, who gathers his profit where he finds it, in this hard world under the law and according to common usage. It is not the individual I attack; it is the system. It is not the man who is bad; it is the law which is bad. It is not the man who is blameworthy for doing what the law allows and what other men do; it is the State which would be blameworthy, were it not to endeavour to reform the law and correct the practice. We do not want to punish the landlord. We want to alter the law. Look at our actual proposal.

We do not go back on the past. We accept as our basis the value as it stands today. The tax on the increment of land begins by recognising and franking all past increment. We look only to the future; and for the future we say only this: that the community shall be the partner in any further increment above the present value after all the owner's improvements have been deducted. We say that the State and the municipality should jointly levy a toll upon the future unearned increment of the land. A toll of what? Of the whole? No. Of a half? No. Of a quarter? No. Of a fifth – that is the proposal of the Budget. And that is robbery, that is plunder, that is communism and spoliation, that is the social revolution at last, that is the overturn of civilised society, that is the end of the world foretold in the Apocalypse! Such is the increment tax about which so much chatter and outcry are raised at the present time, and upon which I will say that no more fair, considerate, or salutary proposal for taxation has ever been made in the House of Commons.

But there is another proposal concerning land values which is not less important. I mean the tax on the capital value of undeveloped urban or suburban land. The income derived from land and its rateable value under the present law depend upon the use to which the land is put. In consequence, income and rateable value are not always true or complete measures of the value of the land. Take the case to which I have already referred, of the man who keeps a large plot in or near a growing town idle for years, while it is 'ripening' – that is to say, while it is rising in price through the exertions of the surrounding community and the need of that community for more room to live. Take that case. I dare say you have formed your own opinion upon it. Mr Balfour, Lord Lansdowne, and the Conservative Party generally, think that is an admirable arrangement. They speak of the profits of the land monopolist, as if they were the fruits of thrift and industry and a pleasing example for the poorer classes to imitate. We do not take that view of the process. We think it is a dog-in-the-manger game. We see the evil, we see the imposture upon the public, and we see the consequences in crowded slums, in hampered commerce, in distorted or restricted development, and in congested centres of population, and we say here and now to the land monopolist who is holding up his land – and the pity is, it was not said before – you shall judge for yourselves whether it is a fair offer or not – we say to the land monopolist: 'This property of yours might be put to immediate use with general advantage. It is at this minute saleable in the market at ten times the value at which it is rated. If you choose to keep it idle in the expectation of still further unearned increment, then at least you shall be taxed at the true selling value in the meanwhile.' And the Budget proposes a tax of a half penny in the pound on the capital value of all such land; that is to say, a tax which is a little less in equivalent than the income tax would be upon the property, if the property were fully developed.

That is the second main proposal of the Budget with regard to the land; and it effects will be, first, to raise an expanding revenue for the needs of the State; secondly that, half the proceeds of this tax, as well as of the other land taxes, will go to the municipalities and local authorities generally to relieve rates; thirdly, the effect will be, as we believe, to bring land into the market, and thus somewhat cheapen the price at which land is obtainable for every object, public and private. By so doing we shall liberate new springs of enterprise and industry, we shall stimulate building, relieve overcrowding, and promote employment.

These two taxes, both in themselves financially, economically, and socially sound, carry with them a further notable advantage. We shall obtain a complete valuation of the whole of the land in the United Kingdom. We shall procure an up-to-date Domesday Book showing the capital value, apart from buildings and improvements, of every piece of land. Now, there is nothing new in the principle of valuation for taxation purposes. It was established fifteen years ago in Lord Rosebery's Government by the Finance Act of 1894, and it has been applied ever since without friction or inconvenience by Conservative administrations.

And if there is nothing new in the principle of valuation, still less is there anything new or unexpected in the general principles underlying the land proposals of the Budget. Why, Lord Rosebery declared himself in favour of taxation of land values fifteen years ago. Lord Balfour has said a great many shrewd and sensible things on this subject which he is, no doubt, very anxious to have overlooked at the present time. The House of Commons has repeatedly affirmed the principle, not only under Liberal Governments, but – which is much more remarkable – under a Conservative Government. Four times during the last Parliament Mr Trevelyan's Bill for the taxation of land values was brought before the House of Commons and fully discussed, and twice it was read a second time during the last Parliament, with its great Conservative majority, the second time by a majority of no less than ninety votes. The House of Lords, in adopting Lord Camperdown's amendment to the Scottish Valuation Bill, has absolutely conceded the principle of rating undeveloped land upon its selling value, although it took very good care not to apply the principle; and all the greatest municipal corporations in England and Scotland – many of them overwhelmingly Conservative in complexion – have declared themselves in favour of the taxation of land values; and now, after at least a generation of study, examination, and debate, the time has come when we should take the first step to put these principles into practical effect. You have heard the saying 'The hour and the man.' The hour has come, and with it the Chancellor of the Exchequer.

I have come to Scotland to exhort you to engage in this battle and devote your whole energy and influence to securing a memorable victory. Every nation in the world has its own way of doing things, its own successes and its own failures. All over Europe we see systems of land tenure which economically, socially, and politically are far superior to ours; but the benefits that those countries derive from their improved land systems are largely swept away, or at any rate neutralised, by grinding tariffs on the necessaries of life and the materials of manufacture. In this country we have long enjoyed the blessings of Free Trade and of untaxed bread and meat, but against these inestimable benefits we have the evils of an unreformed and vicious land system. In no great country in the new world or the old have the working people yet secured the double advantage of free trade and free land together, by which I mean a commercial system and a land system from which, so far as possible, all forms of monopoly have been rigorously excluded. Sixty years ago our system of national taxation was effectively reformed, and immense and undisputed advantages accrued therefrom to all classes, the richest as well as the poorest. The system of local taxation today is just as vicious and wasteful, just as great an impediment to enterprise and progress, just as harsh a burden upon the poor, as the thousand taxes and Corn Law sliding scales of the 'hungry 'forties'. We are met in an hour of tremendous opportunity. 'You who shall liberate the land', said Mr

Cobden, 'will do more for our country than we have done in the liberation of its commerce.'

You can follow the same general principle of distinguishing between earned and unearned increment through the Government's treatment of the income-tax. There is all the difference in the world between the income which a man makes from month to month or from year to year by his continued exertion, which may stop at any moment, and will certainly stop, if he is incapacitated, and the income which is derived from the profits of accumulated capital, which is a continuing income irrespective of the exertion of its owner. Nobody wants to penalise or to stigmatise income derived from dividends, rent, or interest; for accumulated capital, apart from monopoly, represents the exercise of thrift and prudence, qualities which are only less valuable to the community than actual service and labour. But the great difference between the two classes of income remains. We are all sensible of it, and we think that great difference should be recognised when the necessary burdens of the State have to be divided and shared between all classes.

The application of this principle of differentiation of income-tax has enabled the present Government sensibly to lighten the burden of the great majority of income tax payers. Under the late Conservative Government about 110,0000 income-tax payers paid income tax at the statutory rate of a shilling in the pound. Mr Asquith, the Prime Minister, when Chancellor of the Exchequer, reduced the income tax in respect of earned incomes under £2,000 a year from a shilling to nine pence, and it is calculated that 750,000 income-tax payers – that is to say, nearly three quarters of the whole number of income-tax payers – who formerly paid at the shilling rate have obtained an actual relief from taxation to the extent of nearly £1,200,000 a year in the aggregate. The present Chancellor of the Exchequer in the present Budget has added to this abatement a further relief – a very sensible relief, I venture to think you will consider it on account of each child of parents who possess under £500 a year, and that concession involved a further abatement and relief equal to £600,000 a year that statement is founded on high authority, for it figured in one of the Budget proposals of Mr Pitt, and it is today recognised by the law of Prussia.

Taking together the income-tax reforms of Mr Asquith and Mr Lloyd George, taking the two together – because they are all part of the same policy, and they are all part of our treatment as a Government of this great subject – it is true to say that very nearly three out of every four persons who pay income tax will be taxed after this Budget, this penal Budget, this wicked, monstrous, despoliatory Budget – three out of every four persons will be taxed for income tax at a lower rate than they were by the late Conservative Government.

You will perhaps say to me that may be all very well, but are you sure that the rich and the very rich are not being burdened too heavily? Are you sure that you are not laying on the backs of people who are struggling to support existence with incomes of upwards of £3,000 a year, burdens which are too heavy to be borne? Will they not sink, crushed by the load of material cares, into early graves, followed there even by the unrelenting hand of the death duties collector? Will they not take refuge in wholesale fraud and evasion, as some of their leaders ingenuously suggest, or will there be a general flight of all rich people from their native shores to the protection of the hospitable foreigner? Let me reassure you on these points.

The taxes which we now seek to impose to meet the need of the State will not appreciably affect, have not appreciably affected, the comfort, the status, or even the style of living of any class in the United Kingdom. There has been no invidious singling out of a few rich men for special taxation. The increased burden which is placed upon wealth is evenly and broadly distributed over the whole of that wealthy class who are more numerous in Great Britain than in any other country in the world, and who, when this Budget is passed, will still find Great Britain the best country to live in. When I reflect upon the power and influence that class possesses, upon the general goodwill with which they are still regarded by their poorer neighbours, upon the infinite opportunities for pleasure and for culture which are open to them in this free, prosperous, and orderly common wealth, I cannot doubt that they ought to contribute, and I believe that great numbers of them are willing to contribute, in a greater degree than hereto fore, towards the needs of the navy, for which they are always clamouring, and for those social reforms upon which the health and contentment of the whole population depend.

And after all, gentlemen, when we are upon the sorrows of the rich and the heavy blows that have been struck by this wicked Budget, let us not forget that this Budget, which is denounced by all the vested interests in the country and in all the abodes of wealth and power, after all, draws nearly as much from the taxation of tobacco and spirits, which are the luxuries of the working classes, who pay their share with silence and dignity, as it does from those wealthy classes upon whose behalf such heartrending outcry is made.

I do not think the issue before the country was ever more simple than it is now. The money must be found; there is no dispute about that. Both parties are responsible for the expenditure and the obligations which render new revenue necessary; and, as we know, we have difficulty in resisting demands which are made upon us by the Conservative Party for expenditure upon armaments far beyond the limits which are necessary to maintain adequately the defences of the country, and which would only be the accompaniment of a sensational and aggressive policy in foreign and in Colonial affairs. We declare that the proposals we have put forward are conceived with a desire to be fair to all and harsh to none. We assert they are conceived with a desire to secure good laws regulating the conditions by which wealth may be obtained and a just distribution of the burdens of the State. We know that the proposals which we have made will yield all the money that we need for national defence, and that they will yield an expanding revenue in future years for those great schemes of social organisation, of national insurance, of agricultural development, and of the treatment of the problems of poverty and unemployment, which are absolutely necessary if Great Britain is to hold her own in the front rank of the nations. The issue which you have to decide is whether these funds shall be raised by the taxation of a protective tariff upon articles of common use and upon the necessaries of life, including bread and meat, or whether it shall be raised, as we propose, by the taxation of luxuries, of superfluities, and monopolies.

I have only one word more to say, and it is rendered necessary by the observations which fell from Lord Lansdowne last night, when, according to the Scottish papers, he informed a gathering at which he was the principal speaker that the House of Lords was not obliged to swallow the Budget whole or without mincing. I ask you to mark that word. It is a characteristic expression. The House of Lords means to assert its right to mince. Now let us for our part be quite frank and plain. We want this budget Bill to be fairly and fully discussed; we do not grudge the weeks that have been spent already; we are prepared to make every sacrifice – I speak for my honourable friends who are sitting on this platform – of personal convenience in order to secure a thorough, patient, searching examination of proposals the importance of which we do not seek to conceal. The Government has shown itself ready and willing to meet reasonable argument, not merely by reasonable answer, but when a case is shown, by concessions, and generally in a spirit of goodwill. We have dealt with this subject throughout with a desire to mitigate hardships in special cases, and to gain as large a measure of agreement as possible for the proposals we are placing before the country. We want the Budget not merely to be the work of the Cabinet and of the Chancellor of the Exchequer; we want it to be the shaped and moulded plan deliberately considered by the House of Commons. That will be a long and painful process to those who are forced from day to day to take part in it. We shall not shrink from it. But when that process is over, when the Finance Bill leaves the House of Commons, I think you will agree with me that it ought to leave the House of Commons in its final form. No amendments, no excision, no modifying or mutilating will be agreed to by us. We will stand no mincing, and unless Lord Lansdowne and his landlordly friends choose to eat their own mince, Parliament will be dissolved, and we shall come to you in a moment of high consequence for every cause for which Liberalism has ever fought. See that you do not fail us in that hour.

This must rank as one the most radical speeches to have fallen from the lips of a frontbench Minister on the question of taxation in Britain. Churchill had highlighted one crucial truth. Land value is the creation of a community and so belongs to that community.

Churchill was rebuked once again by the King, through Lord Knollys, for suggesting in his speech that the Lords, by rejecting the Budget, would bring about the automatic dissolution of Parliament. 'The King desires me to say', wrote the royal secretary to the Prime Minister, 'that it is painful for him to complain of certain of your colleagues.' What was most painful for the throne was for a Minister to spell out the consequences of a rejection by the Lords. The power to dissolve Parliament was held, nominally, by the King. But Asquith thought this a serious enough departure from the Government line to merit a public rebuke.

Feeling against the Budget in the country was reversed by the work of the Budget League. Churchill, however, was speaking often about principles which the Budget did not put into effect. He was concerned with a broader vision. Evidence of the public mood was provided in the four by-elections held in July. The Liberals won three of them.

A dinner was held on 3 March 1910 at the Commons to honour Sir Henry Norman, who had been the moving force as secretary of the League. Haldane gave the first speech. 'It was', he recalled, 'a stormy period, at a time when people were asking all sorts of questions about details, when their minds ought to have been fixed on principles and the brilliant idea of devising a League to deal only with principles, to send details into the background and imparting to proceedings the full depth of morality.' Churchill expressed the party's gratitude to Sir Henry for inspiring the campaign which expounded Free Trade and the Budget equally. He showed his fighting spirit by reminding his audience that, 'in war when you feel you cannot continue in your position for another minute, and all that is in human power has been done, that is the moment when the enemy is most exhausted, and when one step forward will give you the fruits of the struggle you have borne . . . We have a great party, we have a great leader whom we trust, who will lead us into battle which is deeper in its consequences and darker in its complexities than almost any other political conflict of the last hundred years.'

This tribute to Asquith marked his unexpected entrance and he was persuaded to say a few spontaneous words. 'It [the meeting] has given me the greatest satisfaction to see the spirit with which we are all imbued.'[1]

---

[1] *Times*, 17 July 1909.

11

Political Pilgrimage

The central issue in the General Election of January 1910 concerned the power of the Lords to overturn legislation which had passed the Commons. The people had voted a Liberal administration into office by an enormous majority but had seen them rendered powerless by the implacable Unionist majority in the Lords. The Liberal Government had no formulated policy, the Lords were thinking vaguely about reform of the composition of their House and had no idea that reform of their powers might ever be questioned.

The King disliked moves to destroy an ancient part of the constitution. On 15 December 1909 Lord Knollys told Vaughan Nash, the Prime Minister's Secretary, that the possibility of the King creating sufficient peers to defeat the majority of Unionists was to be reserved until after a second General Election. In other words, this election was to ascertain the people's view of the Budget, and, if they approved of it, the second election could be held on the issue of reform of the Lords.

Lloyd George mocked the peers in a speech at Wolverhampton: 'No testimonials are required [for sitting in the Lords]. There are no credentials. They need not be sound, either in body or in mind. They only require a certificate of birth, just to prove they are first of the litter. You would not choose a spaniel on these principles.'[1]

Generally, the Unionists fought a more effective campaign than in 1906. They were assisted by a number of peers who were engaging in their first General Election – Asquith had introduced a resolution in the Commons to lift an old prohibition, which had barred them from taking part. Balfour's election address was a summary of his party's beliefs. The Liberals, he alleged, were a band of conspirators assailing the Constitution to create single-chamber government. He put himself firmly in the Protectionist camp by stating.

There are those who regard it [tariff reform] as a paradox to say that tariff reform will stimulate home industry. It seems to me a truism. The

---

[1] C. Cross, *Liberals in Power* p. 109.

[government's] way of looking at the problem is illogical and absurd. If it be so desirable that money should be spent on land with slight hope of profit, property in land should not be talked of as an abuse. If it be desirable that small cultivators should give long hours of toil to the development of their holdings, the rewards of possession should be within their grasp.

The main thrust of the Unionist campaign was that the Liberals were conspiring to create single-chamber government. It was formulated most effectively by Lord Cawdor. At Leeds he accused the Government of 'wanting us to copy Bulgaria and Greece in getting rid of a Second Chamber, and Nigeria in its land law'.[1]

Churchill dominated the Election with a series of speeches in Lancashire. Like his speeches in the summer of 1909, they were addressing the principles of the land question, rather than the matters raised in the Budget. His breadth of vision took him into questions which the Budget had not even raised. Asquith wrote in February 1910 to thank him for his efforts in the campaign. 'Your speeches from the first to the last have reached high-water mark, and will live in history.'[2]

Asquith defended Churchill against a further royal outburst by writing to the royal private secretary: 'I hope you have noticed the moderation of tone and the absence of personalities and bad taste – as well as conspicuous ability – which have characterised Winston Churchill's campaign in Lancashire.' These speeches were given between 2 and 12 December 1909. Churchill's campaign in Lancashire was called by the *Manchester Guardian* 'one of the great pilgrimages of English parliamentary history'.

Lancashire had deserted the Liberals over Irish Home Rule in 1885 and in 1900. But the Lancastrian electorate hated the mere idea of protection and since 1903 had reverted to being staunch Liberals. On 6 December in Manchester Churchill said, 'Very important decisions are at stake in the next four weeks in Britain. Do not underestimate the importance of this land question. Here in England we have long enjoyed the blessing of free trade and untaxed bread and meat, but on the other hand we have set against these inestimable boons a vicious and unnatural system of land tenure.'

These speeches were published before the end of that year in a pamphlet, entitled *The People's Rights*. They were offered, said Churchill, in the Preface, to 'my friends in the country, as ammunition passed along the firing line'. His brilliant rhetoric was employed both to pick out the cause of poverty and, at the same time, to herald the mitigation of its effects.

The first chapter, entitled 'The People's Rights', sets out the quarrel between the two Houses of Parliament. 'There is no defence', he stated, 'and there is no answer,

---

[1] *Annual Register* 1909 p. 269.
[2] R. Churchill, *Winston Churchill* vol ii p. 235.

except that the House of Lords has survived out of the past. It is a lingering relic of a feudal order. It is the remainder of a state of things and of a balance of forces which has wholly passed away. I challenge the defenders, the backers, and instigators of the House of Lords – I challenge them to justify and defend before the electors of the country the character and composition of the hereditary assembly.'[1] A more outright remedy to the constitutional problem was meditated by Admiral Lord Fisher. 'Hereditary titles', he bristled, 'are ludicrously out of date in any modern democracy, and the sooner we sweep away all the gimcracks and gewgaws of snobbery the better.'[2] Yet it is less relevant to the nation what the thinking of their Lordships happens to be than what the people themselves think.

> You must realise fully [Churchill continued with the constitutional argument] 'the significance of finance. Upon finance in a civilised nation everything connected with government turns. If the government control the money-bags they control the whole administration of the country. The House that has the power of the purse must be the source and origin of political power. For hundreds of years that power has resided in the House of Commons – that is to say it has resided in the assembly which is selected, which if you do not like you can change, and whose members are amenable to your control and have to come before you to solicit your votes. Now it is suggested that power is also exercised by the House of Lords. I submit to you that it is quite impossible to have two chambers in one country both exercising the power of the purse unless they are both elected and both swing together with the general view of the electors.[3]

Churchill made his points by ridicule quite as keenly as he did by reason.

> What they could not bear is to see the tobacco of the working man taxed by a Liberal Government. That is what upsets Lord Revelstoke. That is what disturbs the Duke of Northumberland. Then they cannot bear to see the whisky which cheers the humble homes of the people until there is very often nothing left to cheer – they cannot bear to see the whisky, 'that liquid food', as it has been described – so cruelly reduced in consumption, that a marked and sensible difference is being made in the habits of the people. That is what breaks Lord Lansdowne's honest heart ... It is inevitable that as a result of the taxes on bread and on meat, and of the great increase of indirect taxation which would accompany these taxes both the consequences to which I have referred would necessarily

---

[1] WSC, *The People's Rights* p, 23.
[2] Lord Fisher, *Records*, p. 73.
[3] WSC, *The People's Rights* p. 27.

follow. But that is not the motive of the House of Lords. They have not been thinking of this. Oh no! Their motive in wanting to put taxes on corn is to unite our great and glorious Empire by the sacred bonds of the food taxation. Their desire to levy import duties on foreign goods is not to relieve themselves of any burden, but to make more work for the working man. Ah! . . . You must remember that the House of Lords have very lately made us a public-spirited offer of the highest importance. They have offered to take over the business of governing ourselves. They have offered to save us all the trouble and worry and vexation and anxiety of governing ourselves. The only thing they do not do is take over is the expense. But everything else is to be done for us. We put the penny in the slot; they do the rest . . . And if any of these distinguished pro-consular administrators were to get wearied of the burden of State, there are 400 or 500 backwoodsmen Peers, all meditating on their estates on the great questions of Government, all studying 'Ruffs Guide' and other blue books, all revolving the problems of Empire and Epsom, everyone of them a heaven-born, God-granted legislator, who knows by instinct what people want, everyone with a stake in the heart of the country, all ready to come forward and fill the gap, if Lord Milner or Lord Curzon should flag.[1]

In fact Lord Curzon, a high priest of high Toryism, took up Churchill's challenge to present the case for the Lords in Lancashire. The viscount has been immortalised in the lines:

> *George Nathaniel, Viscount Curzon,*
> *is a very superior person.*

Doggedly, he followed Churchill's footsteps in Lancashire. In Oldham on 15 December he summarised his argument. It was a great advantage for the Lords not be subject to popular election: to 'the gusts of passion which sweep across the country'. After all the Commons represented only 7.5 million out of a population of 45 million. The hereditary principle, their only election, was natural and observable in professions and vocations. The Lords, could draw on the experience of bishops, ex-MPs, judges, ambassadors, civil servants, 100 military men and 70–80 diplomats. He, Lord Curzon, welcomed working-class representatives in the Commons and would welcome more in his House. Curzon had shone intellectually since his school and university days. He had excelled at everything. He had been viceroy in India. In 1901 he had written to Balfour, 'we are the greatest power in the world.' He firmly believed in the permanence of British rule,

---

[1] Ibid pp. 44–6.

which he stated,' ... will be well for England, better for India, and best of all for the cause of progressive civilisation in general'.[1]

Curzon was an unusual character – not just an ordinary antique, but a collector's piece. Churchill described him thus: 'His facility carried him with a bound into prolixity; his ceremonious diction wore the aspect of pomposity, his wide knowledge was accused of superficiality, his natural pre-eminence was accompanied by airs of superiority.'[2]

The opening of Curzon's election campaign was welcomed by Churchill at Burnley. Yet he derided his initial speech as 'a prize essay in the Middle Ages'. 'All civilisation', said Lord Curzon, quoting Renan, [a French historian] , has been the work of aristocracies.'

> They liked that in Oldham [Churchill warranted]. There was not a duke, not an earl, not a marquis, not a viscount in Oldham who did not feel a compliment had been paid to him. What does Lord Curzon mean by aristocracy? It is quite clear from the argument of his speech that he did not mean nature's aristocracy, the best and most gifted beings in each generation in each country, the wisest, the bravest, the most generous, the most skillful, the most beautiful, the strongest, and the most virtuous. If he had meant that, I think we would probably agree with him ... Again I say this only needs to be stated to be dismissed as absurd. "All civilisation has been the work of aristocracies". It would be much more true to say "The upkeep of aristocracies has been the hard work of all civilisations".[3]

The second chapter was concerned with the Budget.

> The Commons are bound to grant supply, and the Lords are bound to the grant. It is their constitutional duty to assent. They have no right to dissent. How can they dissent? They do not fix the expenditure; no estimates are laid before them; no estimates are examined by them; no financial statement is submitted to them by the executive. They cannot forbid or authorise the spending of a single penny. They have no power to determine how that expenditure can be met. If they destroy the Budget they cannot propose another in its place. They cannot provide a single tax to meet the gap of one they sweep out of existence. Liabilities have been incurred, the House of Lords has even assented to the liabilities by passing the Appropriation Bill for the year. The money must be found. All the House of Lords can do – if they go mad – is to put a stone on the

---

[1] P Moon, *British Conquest and Dominion of India* p. 912.
[2] WSC, *Great Contemporaries* p. 174.
[3] WSC, *The People's Rights* pp. 53–4.

track and throw the train of State off the line, and that is what they are going to do.[1]

The third chapter was concerned with Free Trade, which had been dear to Churchill throughout his political life as a Liberal.

I believe myself that protective tariffs wherever they have been introduced have done great harm. I believe that they have restricted the growth of industries of the nations who have adopted them. I believe that they have been injurious to the poorer classes. I observe the poorer people both in Germany and America bitterly resent the high tariffs under which they live. I believe that these tariffs tend to the corruption of public life and of public men; that they make every town and every part of the country send a member to the legislature not to consider the generous and broad interests of the whole country, but to push the particular line of goods and of manufacture in the place from which he comes. I am quite certain that the high food taxes which prevail in Germany and the United States are a cruel injury to the hard-working people of those countries[2] . . . the rich in every country favour Protection; and in every country they say they favour Protection to benefit the poor.[3]

The fourth chapter, entitled 'The People's Land', was, like the next, 'The People's Welfare', adequately covered in the speeches reproduced in the previous chapter. The speeches on the land were about the principle of the land question which the Budget did not address. The speeches on welfare are delivered in the same powerful, brilliant language but they seemed weak.

Back in his constituency near the end of the election campaign Churchill was welcomed as a great pilgrim. The *Dundee Advertiser* reported on 8 January 1910 that he was given a warm reception and that the audience sang 'The Land Song', amongst others. Churchill asserted three facts. First, the US and Germany had not prevented 'severe fluctuations in trade and cruel unemployment.' Second, the cost of living in these protected countries was higher than in Britain. Third, the quality of work, as judged by exports and the volume of foreign trade, was inferior.

'Land Reform and Free Trade stood together. They stood together with Henry George, with Richard Cobden, and they stood together in the Liberal policy today,' declared Churchill.[4] Indeed these two men had inspired political thinking in his first decade in Parliament.

The other element of the election was the constitutional question. 'The House

---

[1] Ibid p. 63.
[2] Ibid p. 96.
[3] Ibid p. 75.
[4] Speech in Derby 11 Jan 1910, *Land Values* p. 133.

of Lords is face to face with the electors in a furious collision, 'he stated,'and I say that collision must involve a constitutional change' – Churchill was supremely confident. He enjoyed a robust fight about a substantial issue. He thought the rejection of the 1909 Budget by the House of Lords 'was a memorable event in British history which little boys in schools a hundred years hence will read.'[1]

In his election Address he wrote:

> The House of Lords has now reached the final Court of Appeal. Either this election is to settle it once and forever, or all democratic processes of government have come to a full stop and must begin again. As a nation grows in knowledge, numbers and wealth, it should become more broadly master of its own affairs. The British people have reached a point in their history when they must be considered fully entitled to govern themselves ...
>
> The House of Lords which was humble in the days of Disraeli, which was cautious in Lord Salisbury's time, has at last asserted so comprehensible, overwhelming and direct, that no single important measure pressed by the House of Commons, can be carried into law ... But of one matter there is no doubt, the veto of the House of Lords is no aid to our nation. It poisons our politics, it perverts our social balance; it has handspiked our Constitution. They tell me two gentlemen are again to be sent to plead to you Toryism, Protection, and all the muddled malevolence of the Jingo creed.[2]

Churchill won his seat at Dundee in the General Election of 15 January 1910 but the final result was less happy. The Liberal majority of 1906 had vanished; the Unionists had recaptured 116 seats, to total 273 (or two seats less than the Liberals); the Irish Nationalist held 71 seats and the Labour Party 41 and both normally voted with the Liberals. Asquith remained Prime Minister with a comfortable majority in the Commons.

About 58 per cent of adult men had been entitled to vote. South of Humber and Dee rivers became Unionist and the rest of the United Kingdom remained Liberal.

Less radical Liberals blamed Lloyd George and Churchill for the poor election result, which saw the Liberal majority in the election of 1906 almost disappear. Margot Asquith voiced her concern in a letter in February 1910, when the election announcement was decided after polling over three weeks, was complete.

'Private-Burn
Believe me cheap scores, hen-roost phrases & oratorical want of dignity

---

[1] WSC, *The People's Rights* p. 34.
[2] Chartwell Papers, 5/11 26.

is out of date. You have only to say to yrself "Margot Asquith is a little boring & over-earnest but she is right." Loyalty, reserve & character pay the squibs and crackers.

Yrs,

Margot Asquith.'[1]

The Prime Minister offered Churchill the Irish Office. Churchill was prepared to take that office only to prepare for Home Rule. 'The office does not attract me', wrote Churchill. 'There are many circumstances concerned with it which repel me.' In a draft letter, which was not sent, he mentioned the expense, the sea journeys, the atmosphere of ill-will, as its unattractive features. But he thought that Birrel was well placed there. He indicated that he was prepared to consider a move either to the Admiralty or the Home Office. On 14 February 1910 it was announced that he was to become Home Secretary.

---

[1] R. Churchill, *Winston S. Churchill* vol ii p. 333.

12

Parliament Bill

Asquith had played an undistinguished part in the General Election of January 1910. He, was wearied by it and retired to Cannes, in the south of France, as soon as it was over. In his haste, he overlooked an appointment to dine with the King and sleep at Windsor Castle.

After his return he informed the Commons that he had not even asked the King to give a guarantee that he would create sufficient peers required to defeat the Unionist majority in the Lords, because he did not wish to bring the monarch into party politics. 'It was the very worst (speech) I have heard him make,' said Alick Murray, the Liberal Chief Whip. Mastermann recorded that the moral of the Liberal Party sunk. 'I have no vision,' Lloyd George said repeatedly to Masterman. 'I cannot see what to do . . .'[1]

The drama had almost escaped the attention of Punch, but they illustrated Asquith's bleak predicament, after the Election, in a cartoon. He was shown fitted out with armour and lance. Behind the ancient ramparts of the Lords a distant mountain was visible. It was a massive fortress and its flags flew arrogantly in the wind. Asquith, called the 'Liberal champion', looks at his steed, a docile pony that one might expect at the seaside to give grannies a gentle saunter. 'I asked for a charger', complains the Prime Minister, 'and they have given me this.'

The party became extremely depressed. 'Asquith wandered about utterly wretched and restless, like a man conscious that he was facing a situation too big for him ... Winston kept saying to different people. 'We cannot defend intellectually our position on the veto.'[2] Lloyd George and Grey thought of resigning in February 1910.

Sir Harold Nicolson observed that at this time Edward VII 'was a perplexed and apprehensive man'.[3] He told Lord Crewe of his plan that while the Lords would retain the right to attend and speak in their House only 100 would be eligible to vote. The King could not bear to contemplate the creation of a new second chamber.

---

[1] L. Mastertman, *C. F. G. Masterman* p. 158.
[2] Ibid p. 159.
[3] James Pope Hennessy, *Lord Crewe* p. 77.

Home Office

Asquith had been impressed by Churchill's performance in the General Election and had appointed him Home Secretary in February 1910. During Churchill's eighteen months in that office he effected prison reforms to ease the harshness of imprisonment. It was not so much that his mind was stirred to action by official reports, as that his heart was touched by a play, John Galsworthy's *Justice*, in which the actual working of prison conditions on 'the temperament of a sensitive prisoner was brought home with unforgettable poignancy.'[1]

Churchill did not enjoy exercising one duty of the Home Secretary. He received letters of appeal on behalf of prisoners. It was not in his nature to preside over captives and, still less convicted murderers. He found it too distressing. He reviewed 43 cases of capital convictions, confirming the conviction in 22 and granting reprieve in 21. During a debate on capital punishment decades later he remembered, in particular

> the case of a soldier . . ., who in a fit of rage killed his wife . . . After the crime he walked downstairs where a number of little children to whom he used to give sweets awaited him. He took all his money out of his pockets and gave it to them saying, 'I shall not want this anymore.' He then walked to the police station and gave himself up. I was moved by the whole story and by many features in the character of this unhappy man. The judge who tried the case advised that the sentence should be carried out. The officials at the Home Office, with very great experience, suggesting no interference with the course of the law. But I had my own view, and I was unfettered in action in this respect.[2]

The death sentence was converted into a life sentence, but months later the soldier responded to Churchill's merciful decision by committing suicide.

A democratic episode at the Home Office was the siege at Sidney Street, east London, in January 1911. Three anarchists were shooting from a house and they had already killed three policemen. Churchill went to see what was happening. He went, he said, on account of duty. It is difficult to believe curiosity was not his stronger motive.

'The bullets struck the brickwork and ricocheted hither and thither . . . We have since become all too familiar with scenes of this kind, and the spectacle of street fighting has lost its novelty in Europe. But nothing of the sort had ever been seen within living memory in quiet, law-abiding England; and from the point of view of history at least my journey had been repaid.'[3]

---

[1] N. Hilditch, *In praise of Churchill* ch. entitled Home Secretary.
[2] M. Gilbert, *Winston Churchill*, A Life p. 216.
[3] W Churchill, *Thoughts and Adventures* p. 45.

Churchill gave 'covering authority', as he put it, to a fireman not to attempt to put out a fire in the house, for Churchill told Asquith that he had not been prepared to risk 'good British lives in rescuing these ferocious rascals'. As the conflagration descended to the basement Churchill retired to his 'coign of vantage'. When the door was knocked down, two bodies were recovered. Though of the third, 'Peter the Painter', there was no trace.

Churchill was photographed at the scene. The Conservatives mocked him and Balfour told the Commons that Churchill and 'a photographer were both risking valuable lives. I understand what the photographer was doing but what was the Right Honourable gentleman doing?' Churchill wrote in his report to the King that the Conservatives had had 'their mead of merriment'. Though he did concede years later that it had not been 'an altogether unjust reflection'.

Marsh, who had accompanied Churchill to the scene, wrote to a friend about the newsreel film, 'I make a most gratifying appearance, as the central figure of Mr Churchill was directing the operations, at the Palace (a theatre) which was nightly received with unanimous boos and shouts of "shoot him!" '[1]

Masterman burst into Churchill's room at the Home Office later that day and demanded, 'What the hell have you been doing, Winston?' Churchill answered the anxious and censorious interrogant with commanding composure: 'Now, Charlie, don't be croth. It was such fun.'[2]

While Home Secretary Churchill had to deal with the increasing problem of the suffragettes. In principle he was in favour of enfranchising women. But the Commons voted against his Bill in 1911. Asquith pacified them when he promised in 1915 to grant their demands after the First War.

Churchill could resist public campaigns on such issues as free trade. A jute merchant from Dundee, L.K. Caird, offered to finance a campaign for Free Trade. 'I feel', replied Churchill,'the need for continued exertions.'[3] He became Chairman of the National Free Trade Lectures. A series of lantern lectures was arranged over the country. Special exhibitions were used for by-elections. Though the organisation was inspired by a vision or an idea, it lacked the power of the Protectionist campaign. By July it had organised 2414 lectures.

The White Paper of 1909 showed some interesting comparisons during the free trade years.

	1831	1881	1908
Population	24 m	34 m	44.5 m
Paupers	—	90,000	110,000
Average price of wheat	66/4	34/9	44/5
Price of beef (per qtr)		5/6	4/9
Tonnage of registered ships	2 m	6.7 m	11.5 m

---

[1] C. Hassal, *Edward Marsh* p. 171.
[2] L Masterman, *CFG Masterman* p. 184.
[3] Chartwell Papers 2/44, 29.

Such was the record under free trade that Mr Chamberlain and his Protectionists sought to improve upon by tariff reform.

Constitutional Crisis

As Home Secretary Churchill had to brief the King on the situation in the Commons, which was largely concerned with the constitutional crisis. Their Lordships were aware of the need to exhibit a spirit of reform. Lord Lansdowne wrote to Balfour in January 1910 that the Lords accepted 'their admitted faults'. But he felt it was not necessary to go beyond the recommendation of the Rosebery Committee, that the peers should choose a smaller legislative body. In February the Lords were willing to consider reform of their House but they showed no inclination to consider reform of their powers. They passed three resolutions. First, there was a need for a strong and efficient second chamber. Second, their House required reform and reconstruction. Third, the possession of a peerage should no longer bestow the right to sit and vote in their House. Balfour was not carried along in their sudden zeal for reform.

In February 1910 Churchill wrote a Cabinet memorandum on the constitutional crisis. He favoured total abolition of the Lords and its replacement by a new assembly, whose members were elected by the people. But this was rather dry stuff for him. The great Budget issue, with which he inspired the people, had been overtaken by the constitutional issue.

Balfour wrote to the King on 15 February saying, '. . . it would be impossible for the Unionist Opposition to do otherwise than vote against the [1909] Budget as a whole, or, if it came up for separate discussion, those taxes to which they had taken such strong exception both in Parliament and in the country.'

In the Commons Churchill thundered against the Lords. It was, he growled

> . . . a weapon and engine, which has been used by one party to vex, harass and humiliate and finally destroy the other and it has been used so cruelly, so violently, and so bitterly in recent times that there is not a single man on these benches who will consent to hold office on these conditions, except for the sole and express purpose and with the reasonable hope of effecting a permanent change in these conditions.[1]

Speaking in Manchester on 21 March Churchill told his audience there was no hostility to peers, simply because they were peers.

> It is as hereditary legislators that they cannot be supported. Once they have taken their place on equal terms with the general life of their

---

[1] Hansard, col 1580, 31 March 1910, vol. XV.

fellow-countrymen, once they have ceased to be employed to do the squalid work of the great vested interests, I believe they must become a respected and, on the whole, a deservedly popular class.[1]

A Cabinet committee drew up three resolutions to limit the powers of the Lords. They were tabled in the Commons on 21 March. First, the Lords could neither reject or amend a money Bill, which was any Bill designated by the Speaker to be a Bill raising revenue from the people. Second, Bills other than money Bills could be delayed for three parliamentary sessions only. Third, the maximum duration of Parliament would be reduced from seven years to five. These resolutions were embodied in the Parliament Bill. If the Lords rejected these resolutions, Asquith advised the King in Biarritz, Cabinet

> came to the conclusion that it would be their duty at once to tender advice to the Crown as to the necessary steps to be taken to ensure that the policy, approved by the House of Commons by large majorities, shall be given statutory effect in this Parliament. If they found that they were not in a position to accomplish that object, they would either resign office or advise a dissolution of Parliament, but in no case would they feel able to advise a dissolution, except under such conditions as would secure in a new Parliament that the judgement of the people as expressed at the election, would be carried into law.[2]

When the letter was published a few days later, the political situation of Asquith was transformed. The Irish National Members who had been against the Budget, because of the liquor duties, now demanded a commitment to abolish the Lord's veto that same year in order to clear the way for Home Rule in Ireland. They had demanded, before they would assent to the Budget, the reform of the Lords. There was a good deal of Cabinet discussion over the question of the whiskey tax. Lloyd George was prepared to compromise but Asquith stood firm; he regarded such a compromise to be 'a discreditable transaction'. Asquith wrote, 'a good deal of steering was needed to round this rather hazardous point' of Irish reluctance. Now they saw the Prime Minister was minded to take the bull by the horns, and with the removal of the Lords' veto, in order to allow Irish Home Rule through, they passed the 1909 Budget. In fact it went through its three readings in the Lords in a matter of days to become law on 29 April 1910 – a year after its original introduction in the Commons. A deficit of £26 million was adequately covered by uncollected taxes amounting to £30 million. The Budget for 1910–11, which Lloyd George introduced in June, contained no provision for new taxes. The

---

[1] *Times*, 2 March 1910.
[2] R. Jenkins, *Asquith* p. 209.

struggle over the previous Budget, which had started as a financial squabble, now became a constitutional issue.

Asquith was clear that the conclusion of this constitutional question was the great issue before him. But he did not attempt to predict the course. On 4 April he was asked about a procedural detail of the Parliament Act. He answered by repeating four times, 'Wait and see.' It became a label tied around his neck to indicate uncertainty and hesitancy, although it was said with clear confidence.

The King had concealed the fact that he suffered badly from bronchitis. Indeed he was keen to escape the winter in London, which had threatened his health. He had caught a chill in Paris on his way to Biarritz. While Asquith was on a sailing holiday off Portugal he received a telegram from the King's son, George, to say his father had passed away on the evening of May 6.

> I went on deck [recorded Asquith] and I remembered well the first sight that met my eyes in the twilight before dawn was Hailey's comet blazing in the sky ... I felt bewildered and even stunned. At a most anxious moment in the fortunes of State, we had lost, without warning or preparation, the Sovereign whose ripe experience, trained sagacity, equitable judgement, and unwavering consideration, counted for so much.[1]

The late King had 'lived' on a grand scale: plenty of food, drink (a three-bottle-a-day man) and women. He died while at work, which he was determined to keep doing.

Asquith was loathe to push the new King, George V, by demanding an immediate dissolution of Parliament and a royal guarantee on the creation of new peers. George had no experience of political life, as a former naval officer and country man. He had little interest in things urbane or foreign. He was quite simple and Spartan in his tastes. During his first meeting with the King, Asquith suggested that some compromise must be sought with the House of Lords. In June the Cabinet agreed that a constitutional conference be arranged with the Opposition. Thus Asquith, Lloyd George, Crewe and Birrel sat down with Balfour, Lansdowne, Austen Chamberlain and Cawdor at a private meeting in Asquith's room at the Commons.

Asquith allowed Lloyd George to promote his scheme for a coalition with the Unionists. When national difficulties appear insuperable they are either smothered by a Royal Commission or by a coalition of politicians, who speak of national emergencies with the gravity of statesmen, but cling to office like limpets. A conference of eight was formed with four from each side. 'Winston ... is very attracted by it', wrote Lucy Masterman, 'though a rather comic scene, I

---

[1] Lord Oxford and Asquith, *Fifty Years of Parliament* pp. 86–8.

believe, took place when [Lloyd] George asked for his opinion of the arrangement from the point of view of the person left out of it, under which he worked himself up into an astonishing state of indignation, pouring forth rhetorical denunciation of the whole affair.'[1]

Twelve meetings were held before the recess in July and two in October. The Unionists conceded the Government's claim that the Lords should not reject or amend money bills, provided no other measures were 'tacked' onto a money bill. But they would not agree to let through bills of a 'constitutional, organic or structural nature'. The Government agreed that, for example, bills dealing with the Crown or the Protestant Succession should continue to be vulnerable to the veto of the Lords. But under this heading, the Unionists were unwilling to include Irish Home Rule and other matters.

Upon this difference the conference broke up and the Cabinet agreed to another General Election. Asquith sought the guarantee from the King that he would create peers to defeat the opposition in the Lords. The King refused. The Cabinet minuted that, although the guarantee must be given before dissolution of Parliament, its existence need only be made public. The King was still undecided. Lord Knollys advised him to comply with his ministers' advice and also added that the late king was not only minded to ask his advice, but prone to take it as well. But Sir Arthur Bigge, a secretary whom he had employed before his accession, argued against the giving of a guarantee. Certainly Asquith would have resigned and the King would then have to ask Balfour back. The important question in the King's mind was whether Balfour would accept. For if he would not, the King would have to recall Asquith, whom he had effectively dismissed. On 29 April 1910 Lord Knollys had actually prepared a minute to say that Balfour had told him that he would indeed be willing to form a government. But the minute was filed, unread, and Lord Knollys informed the King on 16 November, deliberately misleading him, that Balfour was not willing to act. So the King gave way to Asquith and Lord Crewe, and, reluctantly, gave his word to create sufficient peers after a decisive General Election as would have given the Liberals a majority in the Upper House. In 1913 the King discovered the minute and attached to it a note that he might have acted differently, had he seen the minute in 1911.

Another General Election was called for December 1910. Asquith, Lloyd George and Churchill spoke frequently and forcibly in the election campaign. Asquith concentrated on the constitutional question of whether a chamber facing neither election nor dissolution, should be allowed to frustrate the representative assembly of the people. Lloyd George opened the campaign before a crowd of 4000 at Mile End. He drew applause for recalling his Limehouse speech, held not far away. After a detailed defence of the Budget he set the meeting alight by reminding his audience, 'An aristocracy is like a cheese: the older it is, the higher

---

[1] L. Masterman, *CFC Masterman* p. 164.

it becomes.'[1] At Highbury Churchill referred to the Lords as 'a ludicrous assembly'. But the issues were stale and the electorate were not inspired.

The overall result of the General Election was much the same as the earlier election that year: Liberals 272, Irish Nationals 84, Labour 42 and Unionists 271. The result was little changed from the earlier election in January 1910.

The Parliament Bill was introduced shortly after the parliamentary session opened in February 1911. It provided, first, that money bills were inviolable at the hands of their Lordships, second, that non-money bills became law after being rejected by the Lords in three successive sessions and, third, Parliament should be subject to a five- rather than seven-year term. The effect of these measures would be to remove the power of the Lords to veto legislation approved by the Commons.

As the Bill was grinding through Parliament, the Tories refused to believe the curtain would finally fall to end the drama. Balfour in a speech in the Commons on 2 March 1911 conceded.

'I observe the great body of opinion in this country, represented, I freely admit, by a majority in this House, is of the opinion that the House of Lords went beyond its proper function, and that an adequate reason for altering has arisen.'

But he had in mind reforms about the composition of the other House. He defended the hereditary principle, which had given a monarch to the Empire.

'We ought to see as practical men what we can get out of it. There it is, part of our inherited traditions. There is in conformity with the general feeling of mankind over the greater parts of the earth. Let it be our servant, let it no longer be our master. [Hon. members: 'Here, Here']'[2]

The House of Lords tried to delay the inevitable by introducing a Bill to employ a referendum when the two Houses could not agree, and another provided for a new chamber of reduced numbers, chosen in a variety of novel means. 'These proposals,' wrote Lord Newton, 'which really amounted to a sentence of death upon the most ancient Legislative Chamber in the world, were received by a crowded and attentive House in a dignified if frigid silence and the pallid and wasted appearance of [Lansdowne], who had but lately recovered from a severe illness, seemed to accentuate the general gloom.'[3] Lord Morley effectively killed these hopes of reform when he reminded the House that the Parliament Bill would apply to these new creations, quite as much to the existing order.

The Second Reading of the Parliament Bill in the Commons was wound up by Churchill. I am unable to discover a murmur of protest or title of remonstrance,though I am made conscious occasionally of a yawn of weariness over the unduly prolonged discussion ... [he was] almost

[1] *Annual Register* 1910 p. 238.
[2] Hansard XXII, cols 566–67.
[3] Lord Newton, *Lord Lansdowne* p. 415.

aghast at the Government's moderation. The powers left to the House of Lords would be formidable and even menacing ... One Rt. Hon. Gentleman has told us that the spirit of Henry V is surging in his breast, and the other that he stands with Clive confronting the deadly pistol of the duelist. We may admire the courage all the more because if it has any effect it is the effect which will inure considerably to our advantage. All forms of courage are praiseworthy. But there are two features about the courage that these two Rt. Hon. Gentleman have which deserve the momentary passing notice of this House. First, it is that kind of courage which enables men to stand up unflinchingly and do a foolish thing, although they know it is popular. Second, it is their kind of courage which can only be maintained in the face of danger, but can even shine brightly in its total absence. Mr Jorrocks has described fox-hunting as providing all the glory of war with only twenty five per cent of its danger ... I think no-one has succeeded in manufacturing a greater amount of heroism with a smaller consumption of the raw material of danger than his Rt. Hon. and learned friend.' [F.E. Smith] [He concluded by declaring] We regard this measure as territory conquered by the masses from the classes.[1]

It was a hot summer in 1911 dominated by the splendour of King George V's Coronation in June, a review of the fleet of 165 warships in five columns seven miles long at Spithead, an Imperial Conference and great social events. Briefly the nation forgot the party political manoeuvres. Parliament suspended sittings for a month. Finally on 28 June amendments to the Bill were put down on the Lords' order paper. Accordingly, Asquith asked the King to give his guarantee to create sufficient peers. On 20 July 1911 he wrote to Lord Lansdowne and Balfour as follows:

> I think it courteous and right, before any public decision are announced, to let you know how we regard the political situation.
>
> When the Parliament Bill in the form it has now assumed returns to the House of Commons, we shall be compelled to ask the House to disagree with Lords' amendments.
>
> In the circumstances, should the necessity arise, the Government will advise the King to exercise his Prerogative to secure the passing into Law of the Bill in substantially the same form in which it left the House of Commons, and His Majesty has been pleased to signify that he will consider it to accept and act on that advice.[2]

---

[1] Hansard, 15 May 1910.
[2] Spender and Asquith, *Life of Lord Oxford and Asquith* vol i pp. 312–3.

Meanwhile a split of the Unionist ranks developed. A group led by young Lord Willoughy de Broke, who was known more for fox-hunting than for public speaking, and Lord Halsbury, a former Lord Chancellor aged eighty-seven, rebelled against Lord Lansdowne's increasingly moderate stand. These rebels became known as the 'die-hards' or 'ditchers' to distinguish them from the 'hedgers', as the moderates became known.

The King saw Lord Lansdowne and Balfour to urge them not to compel him to create sufficient peers, by refusing to pass the Parliament Bill in the House of Lords. On 21 July 200 peers met at the house of Lord Lansdowne, who concluded his speech by saying, 'that in his view the more prudent course might be to allow the Parliament Bill to pass'. At last the leader of the Unionists was dealing with fact, rather than fantasy. He judged for himself, without attempting to impose his will that a majority of peers favoured him. He was supported by Balfour and Lord Curzon who had hitherto herded with die-hards. Balfour had tired of the drama. The talk of 'fighting to the last ditch' seemed to him at best 'theatrical', but he really felt it was 'purely for Music Hall consumption.'

Asquith attempted to make a statement in the Commons on 24 July. It was to be the final word in the constitutional drama. It had been foreshadowed by his letter to Lansdowne and Balfour but the Opposition were unwilling to listen to the coffin of all their pretensions being hammered tight. Lord Hugh Cecil and F.E. Smith, with some help from Unionist Members, shouted Asquith down, calling him a traitor, and the murderer of the late king. They were positively demonic. After half an hour the Prime Minister sat down. He had remained calm but outraged. Balfour, who had not tried to moderate the outrageous behaviour of his troops, rose, and while he spoke, absolute silence was preserved by the House. He used no words of censure or apology. Mrs Asquith sent a note begging Sir Edward Grey to save the Prime Minister from the 'cats and cads'. Churchill reported the scene in the Commons to the King. 'The ugliest feature was the absence of any real passion or spontaneous feeling. It was a squalid, frigid, organised attempt to insult the Prime Minister and to prevent debate.'[1]

The Prime Minister was able to answer the accusations of treachery and the like in speaking on a motion of censure of the Government brought by the Opposition in both Houses on the 7 August. He concluded by saying

> ... that I am not the least sensitive to this cheap and ill-formed vituperation. It has been my privilege to serve in close and confidential relation with three successive British Sovereigns. My conscience tells me that in that capacity I have striven to uphold the dignity and just privileges of the Crown. But I hold my office by favour only of the Crown and by the confidence of the people, and I should be guilty indeed of

---

[1] R. Churchill, *Winston S. Churchill Companion*, Pt. 2 p. 1103.

treason if in this supreme moment of a great struggle I were to betray their trust.[1]

Attention now settled on the House of Lords. No-one knew how they would finally vote. The 'ditchers' and the 'hedgers' were bringing up to town their 'backwoodsmen', as Lloyd George called them affectionately. No doubt offended by Lloyd George's jibe that the supreme qualification for lordship was to be born first in a litter, Lord Winster highlighted their traditional skills. He observed that a rural peer knew how to kill a fox, free himself from a disagreeable tenant or an unwanted mistress and he drew the undeniable conclusion that a man possessing these qualities must certainly be able to record a vote. Indeed, his argument was unanswerable.

> In ordinary circumstances [wrote Lord Newton], the House of Lords presents an appearance of polite restraint which seems to represent detachment almost amounting to indifference, and party animosity is concealed under a veil of studied courtesy; but now, for the first time the peers abandoned their habitual restraint and gave vent to the vehement feelings which the situation had provoked. In a word, they behaved like ordinary human beings.[2]

In sweltering heat, as the thermometer reached the 90s, the final debate was held in the Lords on 10 August. The result of the debate was unknown to the last moment. Lord Willoughby de Broke revealed his want of argument when he said, 'You may claim majorities if you like in favour of the Parliament Bill at a dozen General Elections, but you will not alter my view and I do not alter my view and I do not think it will alter the view of Lord Halsbury or those acting with us . . .'[3] The debate was adjourned at midnight.

On the next day Lord Morley intervened at the request of the King. He read the short note stating the King's readiness to create peers and added, 'Every vote given against my motion will be a vote for a large and prompt creation of peers.' The King was surprised by the ardour of the die-hards who convinced themselves the Prime Minister had been bluffing. The debate rumbled on nevertheless. Lord Halsbury spoke just before the vote. His speech was described by Sir Almeric Fitzroy: 'a blunt appeal to blind passion, couched in terms of turgid rhetoric and senile violence.'[4] He spoke when there was a light-headedness in the Chamber.

---

[1] Hansard, vol 29 col 981.
[2] Lord Newton, *Lord Lansdowne*, p. 428.
[3] Hansard, 1911 [Lords], vol 9 col 1,000.
[4] A. Fitzroy *Memoirs*, vol. ii p. 45.

I am not one of those [he tolled like an old bell in a ruin] who regard this as a question to be treated jocosely. I do not think the destruction of this historic House, with all its traditions, with all its powers, and with all the benefits which it has conferred on this country, is a thing to be treated as a climax of fun. It seems to me that is beneath the dignity of the discussion in which we are all engaged and somewhat degrading to the dignity of this House.[1]

The Lords had pressed their cause beyond argument or reason and they had, in the process, revealed that sovereign power in this nation lay not with the Constitution or any of its creatures: it lay with the people.

The Parliament Bill was carried on 10 August 1911 by 17 votes. Indeed the curtain had fallen finally on the fag's and his fag master's 'theatre of compromise'. Wyndham observed with political precision, 'We were beaten by the bishops [thirteen] and the rats [thirty-sevenUnionists].'[2]

Balfour wrote to Lady Elcho from Paris 'Politics have been to me quite unusually odious'. The king told Churchill later that the personal experience of the constitutional crisis had been worse that of the First War.[3] Lloyd George formulated a principle of luminous import when he said 'Liberty owes as much to the foolhardiness of its foes as to the sapience and wisdom of its friends.'[4]

---

[1] Hansard 1911 [Lords], vol 9 col 1071.
[2] Oxford and Asquith, *Fifty Years of the British Parliament*, vol ii p. 13.
[3] WSC, *Great Contemporaries* p. 204.
[4] At a lunch on 3 Dec. 1909 at the National Liberal Club.

13

The End of Radicalism

The first clause of the Parliament Act 1911 – involving bills designated money bills – has never been invoked. The second clause – involving the delay on non-money bills – was used twice by Asquith in the year after the Act was enacted. But this clause was amended by the Parliament Act 1947, which was introduced by Clement Attlee's government to reduce the suspensory period of non-money bills to one year.

Churchill left the Home Office to became First Lord of the Admiralty in October 1911. Lloyd George stayed at the Exchequer and it fell to him to modify some of the reforms which Churchill and he had devised.

The valuation of land was slowed by the requirement to value buildings, fixed machinery and timber. It was quite unnecessary to value these things, since none were liable to tax. In May 1911 a memorandum calling for the completion of valuations was signed by 174 MPs. An unofficial Land Enquiry Committee was set up by Lloyd George in June 1912. By 1912 the estimate that the valuations would be completed by 1914 was seen to be impossible to achieve. Even if they were to be fixed within that time, many by then would be out of date. This achievement is in stark contrast to the industry of a small band who compiled the Domesday Book, during the later eleventh century, in twenty or so years. They had to travel by foot and horseback.

It appeared that the Government had gone cold on the issue and, while professing belief in the cause of land value taxation, did nothing to expedite its implementation. Lloyd George officially opened his 'land campaign' in Bedford in October 1913. He promised a new Lands Ministry to assume land valuation, land-based industries, compulsory purchase, several matters concerning agricultural wages and lettings. The Budget of 1914 attempted to introduce the taxation locally. By 1914 the valuation staff of 14,500 had valued 79 per cent of land and 85 per cent of hereditaments, but only 60 per cent had been awarded a final assessment. In April 1915, Lloyd George suspended the fixation of final land values during the continuance of the War and, in 1918, he scrapped the valuation of land.

During the past ten years, [reported the Select Committee on Land Values in 1919] and especially as a result of the further knowledge gained from the discussions upon the valuations under the Finance Act 1909/10, the rating of site values is no longer regarded so much as a means of raising fresh revenue as a means whereby a stimulus can be given for the better use of land for productive purposes, whether such land be used for building or for agricultural purposes.[1]

The Land Taxes of the 1909 Budget were forecast to raise £500,000 in 1909/10 but in fact they raised only £2725! The sums received by 1918/19 were:

	£
Increment value duty	460,481
Undeveloped land duty	412,019
Reversion duty	262,792
	£1,135,292

By April 1923, after appeals against assessments had been allowed, repayments of land duty paid were as follows:

	£
Increment Value Duty	444,493
Undeveloped Land Duty	154,286
Reversion Duty	239,984
	£838,763[2]

The provisions of the 1909 Budget, as they affected land taxes, were repealed. Austen Chamberlain, then in coalition with the Lloyd George Government, announced this move in the Commons on 25 April 1920. Lloyd George had not even consulted his MPs and was abroad when Chamberlain spoke. The provision for this repeal was contained in clause 49 of the Finance Bill of 1920. In July the Opposition marched through the division lobby singing *The Land Song*.

Indeed the 1909 Budget, in so far as it attempted to tax land, was a fiasco. A Liberal member sitting in Parliament at that time with a sound knowledge of the case wrote: 'The great [Liberal] revival was crushed by the load of disappointment, for the Land Values Bill became a thing of shreds and patches, twisted and tangled out of all shape, unrecognisable, abortive, and disowned by its creators.'[3] The truth is that the 1909 Budget had nothing to do with the recovery of land value by the society. Sir Edgar Harper, the former chief valuer of the Inland Revenue, told an International Conference on Land-Valuation in Edinburgh in twenty years later that, '. . . to say . . . that the Taxation of Land Values has been tried in Britain and has failed, is not only untrue, it is the reverse of the truth!'[4]

---

[1] Select Committee on Land Values 1919, *The Rating of Site Values*.
[2] Hansard, 8 May1923 col 2150.
[3] F. Nielson, *Modern Man and the Liberal Arts* p. 170.
[4] Reported in *Land & Liberty*, [Date].

Clearly Lloyd George did not understand the case for the taxation of land value. He could ridicule the Lords. He could pilot a detailed measure through the Commons. He could pluck an argument out of the air. He could think on his feet. He was a spectacular pragmatist. But the taxation of land values was a fundamental reform. It called for the most rigorous application of reason, justice and courage. It did not lend itself to Lloyd-George's wit, sense of mischief and nimbleness of mind. Haldane, admittedly no friend of land value taxation, wrote that, 'Lloyd George had boundless energy and a quick intelligence, but he was really an illiterate with an untrained mind'.[1]

Churchill had a thorough understanding of the case for the introduction of both free trade and the taxation of land values. He explained the twin measures in the clearest language. Though the Budget of 1909 was a complete failure, his speeches in the 1910 general election still stand today, not as misconceptions of what the Budget intended, but rather as brilliant arguments for first principles. They will stand as classic expositions. Few members of the government front bench in the House of Commons have had the vision and courage to champion two reforms, which would have struck out the root of poverty – the unjust distribution of wealth.

By 1912 the issues were slipping from political life. Churchill's love of the bright lights and ambition allowed the question to fade in his political thinking, as if it had been but a garment, whose season had passed. The First World War finally buried liberal thinking. That fine thinking can be reckoned its enduring victim. The war cast a shadow over the political action of the twentieth century. Political thought has not recovered its pre-war scale. The people have become more heavily oppressed and government has become increasingly powerful, but impotent.

Churchill should be judged by his own lights, which were considerable. Indeed, he was like a glorious torch which shone with a bright light. He had been endowed with great qualities, both as a thinker and an orator. He had deployed them fully on the Liberal front bench. Yet after 1911 he became an ordinary politician during peacetime; distinguished by his command of language but limited by the ordinariness of his political thinking. Never again during peace was he a statesman who could bring light to a dark world and lead a society to espouse grand reform. His place in history is secured as a valiant warrior, but as a champion of peacetime reform, his contribution to political life in his first decade in parliament, has been largely overlooked.

In his book, *Thoughts and Adventures*, published in 1928, Churchill wrote:

It is inevitable that frequent changes should take place in the region of action. A policy is pursued up to a certain point; it becomes evident at last that it can be carried no further. New facts arise which render it

[1] A.J.P. Taylor, *Lloyd George 12 Essays* p. 67.

obsolete; new difficulties, make it impracticable. A new and possibly the opposite policy assert themselves with overwhelming force. To abandon the old policy it is often necessary to adopt the new.[1]

Indeed politics is subject, not to enduring principles, but to temporary crises, passing fashion and it acquires in the fast-moving world a superficiality, which, in turn, becomes the veneer of injustice and misery. Principles founded in justice are the pillars of freedom. Without them a politician, particularly one who once held them, is a sad figure, like a conjuror without a wand or an audience.

The truth is, sadly, the British people were not with Churchill after February 1910 when the Budget was replaced by the constitutional struggle. It was as if the seed of the fruit had been rejected in favour of the husk. Though it was necessary to terminate the power of the 'feudal relic', the House of Lords, the underlying issue that led to that reform was immensely more important than the Parliament Act. The Act concerned Westminster, whereas taxation concerns the entire people.

However, it is simplistic to pretend Churchill was caught in a private dilemma of either choosing reform of causes or mitigating the effects of causes, which have not been eradicated. For that dilemma confronted the nation and Churchill merely followed, as a public servant, where public opinion directed: towards the make-believe world of mitigation.

Churchill estimated Asquith as the most excellent Prime Minister in peacetime. Asquith was a rare man in politics; he had a brilliant mind and was possessed of unshakeable integrity. Such qualities reminded Churchill of a great judge. Asquith, however, understood only a little of the case for land value taxation, as he made clear in a speech at Paisley several years later.

> I think as I have always thought, that land should contribute – not in the sense of a penalty – on grounds of equity and justice, contribute with other forms of property and other forms on income to the general burden which ought to fall upon the shoulders of the whole community.[2]

Though he had nibbled at the land question and lacked a grasp of the problem, he failed to deploy creative or imaginative thought. The budget, he argued, sought to prevent the windfall increment in land value falling into private hands. It was a vague notion. Asquith fell into the trap of half-defining the cause of a problem and assuming that it would be overcome by the Government's policies. His error was, first, in the diagnosis of the evil of private ownership of land value and, second, in the remedy. The measure had demanded a breath of vision which was wanting in the Prime Minister and Cabinet. Churchill had that vision.

---

[1] Under chapter, *Consistency in Politics*.
[2] *Daily News*, 28 January 1920.

Asquith might have noticed that while Churchill was speaking of the principle of the Chancellor's measures, Lloyd George was disregarding them. The Government in 1908 had put its future on the next Budget. That it was, as far as land value taxes were concerned, a complete failure must be reckoned as the failure of his Government. Liberalism had been a refuge of freedom during the nineteenth century but it foundered as an outdated fashion in the twentieth century. The budget of 1909 was the zenith of Liberalism and, thereafter, it has been all downhill into enveloping unimportance. Responsibility for the decline of Liberalism must be borne by Asquith, who allowed such an important measure to be wrecked by Lloyd George.

When free trade was undermined by the dishonesty of the Conservative protectionists, Churchill raised no demur; when it was thrown aside in 1931, Churchill was often absent from the Commons. Churchill's political career between the wars became dominated by war; as it had been dominated before 1911 by peacetime reforms.

The case for land value taxation was taken up for a time by the Labour Party. Philip Snowden, the Chancellor of the Exchequer in 1924 and 1929–31, stated that, 'he was not deterred by Mr Lloyd-George's comparative failure . . . At the first opportunity he would submit financial proposals for the taxation of what was generally called the unearned increment on land.'[1] Snowden introduced a measure to impose a 1d in the £ on capital values of land in his Budget of 1931. Unhappily a crisis of confidence overtook the City. A National Government was formed under Ramsay MacDonald. The Tories pressed for the introduction of protection and the repeal of the land value taxation clauses in the 1931 Budget. Against undertakings given to Snowden by MacDonald – that the 1931 land tax would stand – it was repealed in 1934. Austen Chamberlain, still a staunch Tory and still a sharp-eyed undertaker of radical thinking, finally pushed the Prime Minister to give way and break his undertaking given to Snowden not repeal the land valuation clauses.

Churchill's virtue would not allow him to recant his former faith, as other protagonists of the land question had done. In 1917 Churchill told a heckler in Dundee, 'I have made speeches by the yard on land values, and you know what a strong supporter I have always been of that policy.'[2] On 21 April 1944 he told the House of Commons, 'I have no intention of passing my remaining years in explaining or withdrawing anything I have said in the past, still less in apologising for it . . .'

There are two principal reasons for adding this period of Churchill's radicalism to his considerable archive. The first reason is concerned with Churchill himself. In his whole political life he was like an eagle with two large wings unfurled at different times in peace and then in war.

---

[1] *The Times*, 17 May 1924.
[2] R. Hellman, *Henry George Reconsidered* p. 172.

His record in war is well-known. As he rode to Buckingham Palace on 10 May 1940, after being appointed Prime Minister, he was 'conscious of a profound sense of relief. I felt as if I was walking with destiny, that all my past life, had been a preparation for this hour.' Three day later he told the House of Commons, 'I have nothing to offer but blood, sweat and tears.' Within three weeks the defence of Western Europe was routed. 250,000 British and 110,000 French troops were evacuated from Dunkirk. Churchill seized victory out of this terrible reverse. 'There was a white glow, overpowering, sublime, which ran through our island from end to end.'[1] That was followed immediately by the Battle of Britain which lasted until the following June. After Dunkirk Britain stood alone. Her spirit, defiance and determination to fight until 'each one lay choking in his own blood'[2] was delivered by Churchill as though he were a beast deep in a forest made ferocious by a wound. His speeches constituted the main defence against the vileness of Nazism and Russia opened the Eastern front in July 1941 and the entry of America five months later. Throughout the democratic world Churchill stood as a defender f democracy. That aspect of Churchill's life has been thoroughly unearthed. The inspiration imparted to the people of his time was immense and it will inspire their offspring forever.

Churchill's speeches delivered in the first decade were directed at the cause of injustice were remarkable. He captured the spirit of radicalism which is often overlooked as an important feature in Edwardian Britain. It was recognised that the Poor Law regime had failed over three centuries to disguise poverty and that it had become a condition afflicting the mass of society. Churchill had the courage to embrace the reform of this inhuman and completely unnecessary condition. It had lingered as a darkening shadow in Britain for at least five centuries. It appears that no government minister had taken the eradication of causes more seriously than in its mitigation. A few had muttered about poverty as the fruit of injustice and figures like Thomas More had railed impotently against land enclosure but none had concentrated the courage to speak clearly about its cause. Though comparatively young, Churchill touched the top rung in peace as he would in war.

The cause of poverty is something the House of Commons treats with the temerity of a child handling hot coals. The cost of trying to sweep it under the carpet has been immense. Churchill showed that the political pose of compassionate treatment of the poor, the devotion of billions of state money to the poor and the labelling of this vast experiment at buying poverty off as 'the welfare state' are as unjust and cruel as poverty itself. Indeed, Churchill had lifted the lid off a can of worms. His stand during the first decade of this century applies with even greater force at the end of the century. The question is not whether the

---

[1] P. Brendon, *Winston Churchill* p. 81.
[2] *Churchill – A profile* edt. P. Stansky p. 147.

able-bodied individual should look themself and their family. Plainly only a few rich people fund their education, health and retirement. The question remains, as it appeared to Churchill, why cannot all individuals do so? Or why can they not enjoy a prosperous and creative life which their efforts merit? Churchill believed that injustice was the reason and that it should be lifted by parliament through taxation. That is a contribution to the political thought of democracies of singular importance. Indeed, it has transcended most of parliament's thinking about matters concerning the distribution of wealth.

The question Churchill raised in his first decade in Parliament remains. He asked, in effect, what is the general cause in society of poverty among able-bodied persons. That alone contains as large a question in peacetime as survival does in war. Why should such a noble creature as man live under injustice when not at war?

To thoroughly understand Churchill as a political character regard must be paid to his greatness in peace as well his memorable wartime record. He did not just shine with exceptional brilliance during the Second World War. But his political career during peace time after the First World War was unremarkable. When he embraced the large issues of free trade and taxation during the first decade in Parliament he was a striking figure but when he forgot these principles, his light went out and he appeared as unremarkable as the generality of politicians more concerned for popularity than justice and freedom. The Second World War summoned Churchill from the ordinariness of political life.

The second reason is that this period shows something about political thought. The people of Britain, particularly in Scotland, were politically alive and intelligent in the last decades of the nineteenth century and the first of this century. Their thought was robust and concerned with the birthright of every individual to earn the full measure of their efforts in order to enable personal and family responsibilities to be discharged. Churchill was stimulated by the thinking of the electorate to master their case and circulate their thoughts so beautifully and so powerfully. His audience were rapt – that much is evident in the photographs of his meetings – and were aware that a statesman had spoken. But the speeches were delivered in such a way that it was as if their own thoughts had been borrowed, brightened and put in a larger frame. The substance of politics is sometimes on rare occasions, like war or emergencies, concentrated at Westminster. But in peace it is present more in the minds of the electorate. If the people do not think clearly and profoundly neither will parliament, for it is just a mirror of the people. It would a great mistake to mourn the loss of Churchill at the helm of state or to hope for deliverance from a Prime Minister or government. For the robust individualism of political thought died out during the build-up of the First War. Indeed it has proved its most enduring casualty. Before there was a desire for radical reform to remove the cause of poverty and after a willingness to cover it up with schemes of mitigation. Churchill after that war was, judged against his former lights, remarkably ordinary duing peace. The statesman was eclipsed by the party politician. As Chancellor of the Exchequer, with the armoury of taxation at his disposal, he proved a failure and allowed free trade to be replaced by protectionism. His new party also interred the taxation of land value introduced by Snowden in 1931, for injustice is, along with protectionism a corner stone of reactionary politics. In fact it can be said that as a peacetime politician after the First War, Churchill was a failure. His passion had died with that of the people. It is idle to pull a figure like Churchill down and ignore the people's fall from grace. For both rose and fell together.

In 1910 Britain gained reform of the House of Lords, although that was really only the small change of a much larger campaign. Yet the nation has the speeches of Churchill to remind itself that an alternative to the mitigation of poverty is the removal of its cause. How wrong Churchill was when he predicted that the rejection of the budget by the House of Lords would go down as a 'memorable event in English history of which all the little boys in schools a hundred years hence will read.'[1] Asquith shared his belief and wrote: 'Your speeches have reached high-water mark, and will live in history.'[2] That episode, which revealed much about the political thinking of Britain and about the statesmanship of Churchill, has been quietly buried by forces which prefer politics to remain dull, docile and superficial.

---

[1] WSC, *The Peoples' Rights*, p. 34.
[2] R. Churchill, *Winston S. Churchill* vol 11 p. 363.

Index